The Art of Monetary Policy

The Art of Monetary Policy

Lessons from Sun Tzu for Central Banks

Kristin Forbes

The MIT Press
Cambridge, Massachusetts
London, England

The MIT Press
Massachusetts Institute of Technology
77 Massachusetts Avenue
Cambridge, MA 02139
mitpress.mit.edu

The MIT Press would like to thank the anonymous peer reviewers who provided comments on drafts of this book. The generous work of academic experts is essential for establishing the authority and quality of our publications. We acknowledge with gratitude the contributions of these otherwise uncredited readers.

This book was set in Stone Serif and Stone Sans by Westchester Publishing Services. Printed and bound in the United States of America.

Library of Congress Cataloging-in-Publication Data is available.

ISBN: 978-0-262-05233-7

10 9 8 7 6 5 4 3 2 1

EU Authorised Representative: Easy Access System Europe, Mustamäe tee 50, 10621 Tallinn, Estonia | Email: gpsr.requests@easproject.com

Contents

Series Foreword

The Swiss National Bank is grateful to Kristin Forbes for writing this book in which she revisits and develops the ideas presented in her Karl Brunner Distinguished Lecture of October 3, 2024. The series of books associated with the Karl Brunner Distinguished Lecture explores topics of key importance to central banking.

The Karl Brunner Distinguished Lecture Series, which is organized by the Swiss National Bank and takes place annually in Zurich, honors eminent monetary theory and policy thinkers whose research has influenced central banking. The scope of the lecture series reflects the attention Karl Brunner devoted to monetary economics, his belief in the need to advance theoretical and applied analysis in this field, and in particular his concern for the policy relevance of economic science.

Martin Schlegel, Chairman of the Governing Board

1 Introduction

The art of war is of vital importance to the State. It is a matter of life and death, a road either to safety or to ruin. Hence it is a subject of inquiry which can on no account be neglected.

—Sun Tzu, *The Art of War*, Chapter 1, Principles 1 and 2

Many of Sun Tzu's military insights from the fifth century BC could have been written for central banks today. Monetary policy is of "vital importance to the State," and over the past two decades central banks have played prominent roles in stabilizing economies and finding the "road" to "safety" instead of "ruin." Fighting the 2008 global financial crisis and 2020 COVID-19 pandemic has been as complicated, contentious, and costly as many military battles, forcing central banks to innovate and develop a multifaceted set of new weapons that have substantially expanded the banks' authority and reach. This has, not surprisingly, raised questions about the utilization and effectiveness of these new tools and broader powers. An "inquiry . . . can on no count be neglected"—not only to understand the past, but also to plan for the future, as central banks will inevitably be drafted into service during the next economic and financial conflagration. In a world of higher debt levels, tightly interconnected markets, and rising geopolitical tensions, effective responses by central banks will be even more critical as the casualties from miscalculations will only grow over time.

In this book, I attempt to perform this "inquiry." I draw lessons for central banks from the last two, tumultuous decades and use these insights to provide suggestions for how central banks can improve their responses and support more resilient economies in the future. To do so, I draw on the writings of the Chinese philosopher Sun Tzu, a military strategist whose principles have not only endured for 2,500 years, but have also been applied to a wide range of disciplines and personal life.[1] My conclusions echo those of Sun Tzu; the decisions that lead to success are more of an art than a science, but should be based on several core tenets. For central banks, this "art of monetary policy" should involve six principles: (1) careful planning; (2) accepting the inevitability of external shocks; (3) establishing a strong tactical position; (4) combining different weapons for the specifics of each situation; (5) maintaining flexibility to quickly adapt when the situation evolves; and (6) evaluating the short- and long-run trade-offs.[2] There is no single action, tactic, or equation that can guarantee victory, but following this set of guiding principles can greatly increase the odds of accomplishing your goals (and of avoiding the worst losses and outcomes).

After an unusually tumultuous two decades, this is an opportune time for this type of evaluation of best practices for monetary policy. Figure 1.1 places these last two decades in the historical context, highlighting the economic instability which forced central banks to innovate, respond aggressively, and expand into new territory, without the benefit of time to carefully analyze each strategy. The figure shows median growth in real GDP (gross domestic product) per capita from 1900 through 2022, for fifty-eight countries and

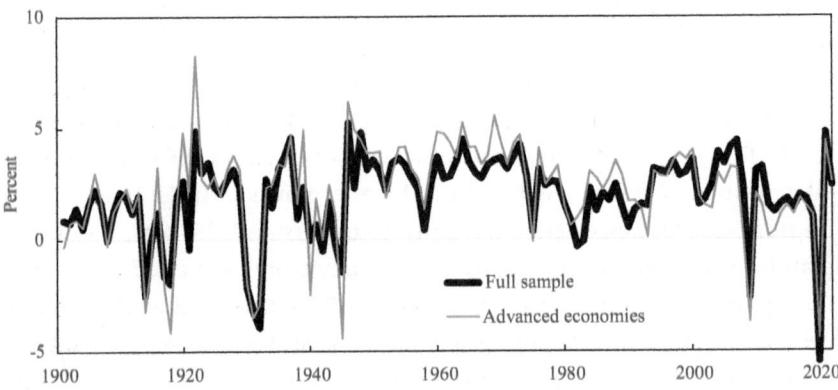

Figure 1.1
Median growth in real GDP per capita: 1900–2022. *Note*: Graph shows median growth in real GDP per capita in 2011 US$. Full sample is the fifty-eight countries with data for 1950 and 2022; advanced economies is a subsample of twenty-four advanced economies based on IMF definitions in 2022. *Source*: Data to calculate growth rates is from the Maddison Project Database (2023), with information in Bolt and van Zanden (2024).

a subset of advanced economies.[3] In both groups, the collapse in GDP per capita experienced during the great "battles" of the 2008 global financial crisis (referred to hereafter as "the GFC") and the 2020 COVID-19 pandemic (referred to hereafter as "the pandemic") was unlike anything experienced over the previous half century. In fact, the median collapse in GDP per capita was greater in 2020 than during any year of World War I, World War II, or the Great Depression. This instability was particularly surprising after decades of reduced economic volatility and the "Great Moderation" over the two decades before the GFC. It is understandable that governments and central banks felt the need to respond in force—even if this meant experimenting with untested battle strategies and substantially expanding their reach into new terrain.

What can we learn from these new and aggressive strategies used in the great battles of the GFC and the pandemic? After the introduction, each of six chapters applies one of the principles from Sun Tzu to evaluate central bank responses during this period of hyperactivity and provide suggestions for improvement. The final chapter brings together these lessons and insights to put the role of central banks in the broader context of what they can (and cannot) realistically accomplish.

The first principle applied from *The Art of War* is the importance of laying plans well in advance in order to prepare for the next battle. The interconnection of global markets combined with recent financial innovations allow shocks to propagate much more quickly and violently than in the past. Policymakers may have little time to craft a response. Detailed contingency planning must be done ahead of time. A second principle is acceptance of the power and inevitability of Sun Tzu's "heaven," that is, external shocks. Their role has grown over time and can have first-order effects on financial markets and the broader economy. Central banks should adjust their strategies, mandates, and goals to accept and adapt to these forces over which they have no control. A third principle is the need to work within the constraints of "earth" and the "terrain" to establish a strong tactical position to face these challenges. With careful planning, such as establishing strong macroprudential defenses, economies can build a more resilient starting point, such that they are better fortified against the large and "heavenly" external shocks.

A fourth principle is the importance of appropriately combining various tools, weapons, and methods in order to maneuver effectively in the face of each challenge. The appropriate blend and timing of tools, weapons, and methods vary based on the situation—with recent lessons for central banks on when it is best to solely adjust policy interest rates, when it is best to solely adjust balance sheets, and when these tools can be used simultaneously (and even simultaneously in opposite directions in some circumstances). There can be important advantages of having multiple weapons in your arsenal—if used appropriately. A fifth, and closely related, principle is the need to maintain flexibility and be able to quickly modify your tactics in order to adapt as the situation evolves, especially as shocks can transmit in new and unexpected ways. As central banks have experimented with new tools, they have learned that certain combinations can restrict their ability to adjust when the environment changes.

A final principle is the importance of accounting for the resources and costs of different strategies over different time horizons in order to fully assess the trade-offs. Some tactics used over the last two decades were seen as a "free lunch" a priori, but generated substantial costs ex post when the battle was won (particularly quantitative easing). This is a reminder of the need to account for broader contingencies and outcomes when assessing trade-offs. Each of these six principles is important in isolation, but also in their many interactions, such as the risks from heavenly shocks reinforcing the need for building a strong tactical position and other careful advance planning.

What would Karl Brunner (the renowned Swiss economist who is honored in this lecture series) think of this analysis and these lessons? Brunner would undoubtedly be delighted to engage in this discussion of monetary policy and the optimal strategies for central banks. He would also undoubtedly be delighted to see the importance placed on making decisions under uncertainty—a key theme of his research (as for Sun Tzu). A central banker operating in a highly integrated world subject to global shocks must be as ready for surprises and different contingencies as a general planning for battle. As a founding member of the Shadow Open Market Committee (which provides advice to the U.S. Federal Reserve on its policy decisions), Brunner would also likely be delighted to see a fellow economist offering advice to central banks (including criticism of some past decisions).

There are also parts of this discussion, however, about which Brunner would likely be less enthusiastic. Brunner believed in simple rules for monetary policy, rather than discretion. He was a monetarist—someone who believed that central banks should announce and focus on a target for the growth in the money supply. I doubt he imagined, even in his most speculative moments, the expansion of central bank tools and powers that has occurred over the last two decades. But Brunner also did not experience the severe economic and financial turmoil in 2008 and 2020 (figure 1.1)—both of which occurred after his death in 1989—and which triggered this innovation and extension of central bank powers. It is a shame we will never learn how these events might have changed his preference for a more limited role of central banks.

Finally, even if Karl Brunner would not have supported these unprecedented responses, his intellectual curiosity would undoubtedly have led him to agree that a careful analysis of central bank actions over the last two decades is merited. What did they do well? What could they do better next time? Even though the more activist strategies adopted by central banks over this period were far from perfect, their flexibility, creativity, and willingness to experiment played a critical role in helping stabilize financial systems and supporting broader economic recoveries. While central banks and governments would undoubtedly prefer not to revisit many of the emergency responses from the last two decades, many of these strategies will likely be considered again whenever the next conflagration occurs—just as countries seek to avoid armed conflict, but often find themselves mired in military engagements when there are no better options. The relative peace existing today is the opportune time to use Sun Tzu's principles to draw lessons from the last two decades and better prepare for future battles.

2 Laying Plans: Preparing for the Next Financial Battle

Sun Tzu begins his book with the importance of "laying plans" in advance of any confrontation.

> Now the general who wins a battle makes many calculations in his temple ere the battle is fought. The general who loses a battle makes but few calculations beforehand. Thus do many calculations lead to victory, and few calculations to defeat: how much more no calculation at all! (Sun Tzu, *The Art of War*, Chapter 1, Principle 26)

The last two decades have also highlighted the importance of laying plans for central banks, particularly for periods of financial stress when a rapid and credible response is of the essence. This chapter outlines what central banks have learned over this time frame and then provides some broad suggestions for facilitating effective planning in the future—many of which are developed in more detail in subsequent chapters.

Lessons from the Last Two Decades

Central banks must develop two sets of strategies: for "normal" times (when central banks are focused on achieving their mandates for price stability or economic activity, or both) and for "crisis" periods (when markets are dysfunctional and the financial system under such severe stress that central banks prioritize financial stability mandates).[1] Planning for crisis periods is where central banks have learned the most over the last two decades, but also where additional progress is most urgent.

Laying plans for normal periods is more straightforward (at least relative to crisis periods). This does not necessarily imply pre-committing to a path for monetary policy, but instead, establishing a transparent framework for how monetary policy decisions are made and combining this with regular communication on the economic developments and considerations that will influence these decisions. This can involve guidance on the stance of monetary policy in the near term, or on specific economic variables or risks that will determine the stance of monetary policy over the short or medium term. These types of plans, however, should also include some flexibility in case the economic situation does not evolve as forecast, an important consideration discussed in more detail in chapter 3 (on the role of "heaven" in generating surprises) and in chapter 6 (on the importance of being able to adjust tactics quickly).

Laying plans for crisis periods is more complicated. Predicting what will trigger the next crisis and how it unfolds is extremely challenging—if not impossible—and there is often much less time to craft a response. For example, although a number of people identified weaknesses in the U.S. housing market in 2007, and some even worried about contagion to major financial institutions, no one predicted the manner in which the bankruptcy of one financial institution (Lehman Brothers) would trigger the collapse of a major insurance company (AIG), runs on money markets, and the sharpest global recession since the Great Depression. Similarly, although some epidemiologists worried about a global pandemic before 2020, no central bankers (to my knowledge) predicted how quickly a virus could spread and trigger lockdowns around the world, a collapse in global supply chains, and disfunction in the world's most liquid financial market (for U.S. Treasury securities). These recent experiences, however, highlight that many of the key principles for planning during normal times still apply during crises: establish a transparent framework for how central bank decisions are made and combine this with effective communication about the economic developments and considerations that influence these decisions.

These recent experiences also highlight an additional component of planning that is even more critical during crises: the ability to respond quickly. This includes advance planning about the types of facilities and programs that may need to be created, including any preparations that allow them to be deployed rapidly. When liquidity evaporated and financial markets froze up in March 2020, one reason why central banks were able to respond so quickly with a range of facilities (discussed in more detail in chapter 5) was their ability to draw from the programs developed just over a decade earlier in response to the GFC. Having a blueprint that was still fresh—and people who had been involved in implementing these programs in the last crisis—allowed central banks to quickly launch programs targeting critical market stresses. Even if the programs previously used were not believed to have enough firepower in the spring of 2020, it was much easier to expand the scale, speed, and scope of previous facilities than to design and implement new programs from scratch (English, Forbes, and Ubide 2024). This prior experience also allowed central banks to focus on programs that had already been proven to have the greatest impact.

This speed in responding to a financial crisis is critically important because a collapse in one major financial institution can quickly spread to other institutions, the broader domestic financial system, and financial systems around the world. The corresponding "doom loops" and "diabolic loops," if not quickly addressed, can increase a sovereign's credit risk and even threaten the solvency of a nation.[2] Responding quickly can limit the amplification of the initial financial distress, avoiding these death spirals that can undermine viable institutions, broader financial systems, and entire economies.

Potentially even more disconcerting, technological advances have increased the speed by which bank runs, financial crises, and these doom loops can occur—leaving central banks even less time to respond and battle contagion. The increased use of online banking and improvements in electronic payment systems allow consumers and companies to withdraw deposits from banks much more quickly than in the past. Social media can amplify the speed at which news and rumors spread, causing large, connected networks to quickly adjust financial positions in a similar way.

The unprecedented speed of the 2023 collapses of Silicon Valley Bank and Signature Bank provides a chilling example of how these technological developments have amplified the speed of bank runs.[3] During the GFC, starting in 2008, the deposit runs that triggered the two largest U.S. banking collapses (of Washington Mutual and Wachovia) occurred over a period of sixteen and nineteen days, respectively, during which the banks experienced "what were called 'massive' deposit runs at the time, involving 4.4 percent and 10 percent of deposits, respectively."[4] In contrast, the 2023 collapses of Silicon Valley Bank and Signature Bank occurred after deposit runs of about a day, over which 87 percent and 29 percent of deposits, respectively, were withdrawn.[5] When rumors can spread quickly on social media, and individuals can withdraw deposits with a click on their laptop instead of having to travel to the institution and wait in a long line, financial institutions can become insolvent in hours and even minutes rather than weeks.

These poignant lessons that individual institutions can collapse and generate financial contagion more quickly than just a decade ago suggest that central banks should prioritize Sun Tzu's advice of planning for the next battle. Even if central banks are starting with a better plan for addressing severe financial stress than anything that existed before the GFC, there is still more work to be done. Not only may the next battle take a different form—the perennial challenge with financial crises—but also it could easily erupt and unfold even more quickly.

Laying Plans: Suggestions for the Future

Given these challenges and uncertainties, how can central banks improve their planning for the next financial crisis? Key components include preparing for large global shocks and strengthening the resilience of financial systems so that they can better withstand these shocks (see chapters 3 and 4 on the roles of "heaven" and "earth"). Key components also involve careful development and evaluation of the tools that are available, including how different strategies interact and how quickly they can be adjusted (discussed in more detail in chapters 5 and 6). These components, however, may still not be enough when the next crisis strikes.

Central banks should also actively plan for a broader range of emergency liquidity and market support facilities that could be quickly deployed in response to different forms of financial stress (including for different markets and non-bank financial institutions). This does not mean that these emergency facilities should be used regularly. In fact, ideally, they would not be used at all. Nonetheless, more advance planning should be done than is the current practice so that a facility could be quickly launched when markets stop functioning and speed is of the essence. Developing structures and guidelines a priori should improve the likelihood that decisions are made according to central bank mandates and are not politicized. It should also prevent rushed decisions that often lead to less well-designed programs and higher costs ex post (as discussed in chapter 7).

Designing these types of programs and facilities is not straightforward. It is necessary to balance a sufficiently large size and scope of support to be credible and stabilize markets while minimizing the costs and distortions to market pricing, including reducing moral hazard (i.e., when institutions do not appropriately account for risks or price them due to an expectation of government support). The design of programs and facilities should include strict and well-defined criteria for access, including the requirement that they are only available when there are risks to the entire financial system (and not individual institutions) and that users pay a penalty fee. These trade-offs merit careful thought. Detailed designs of these types of programs and facilities are beyond the scope of this book, especially as any plans should be tailored to address the specific characteristics and vulnerabilities of each country.[6] Nonetheless, there are several tenets which should be included in these plans:

(a) the individuals (or group) who decide whether to enact these facilities and programs; this could be some type of Financial Policy Committee that includes market expertise and is distinct from the Monetary Policy Committee (although it may involve some overlap in membership);[7]

(b) the criteria that trigger the use of these facilities;

(c) the types of institutions (i.e., banks, primary market dealers, etc.) that have access to a particular facility;

(d) the types of collateral and/or institutional criteria (i.e., criteria for solvency) that allow the institutions to access each facility;

(e) how institutions using each facility are charged; this should involve a penalty cost that deters use of the facility when markets are functioning normally and mitigates concerns about moral hazard; and

(f) when the program would be ended and how any holdings would be wound down; the priority should be to exit quickly, make any facilities temporary, and unwind any purchases as soon as possible (without creating market disturbance).

While these are only broad concepts, Buiter et al. (2023) provides a thoughtful and more detailed set of proposals, drawing on the experience of the liquidity and market support packages used in response to the pandemic. The facility developed by the BoE in response to the Liability-Driven Investment (LDI) crisis in 2022 is also a useful model; it incorporates most of the above criteria and benefited from thought and discussion in advance (Bailey et al. 2020). Kashyap (2024) is also a useful starting point for an institutional arrangement to oversee these types of programs; it proposes a "Purchase Facilities Committee (PFC)" to implement emergency financial support programs. The collapse of Credit Suisse in March 2023 provides a useful case study for how to improve resolution plans for winding down large global banks.[8] Ongoing work by the European Systemic Risk Board, Financial Stability Board, International Monetary Fund, and Bank for International Settlement also includes helpful discussion of lessons learned and paths forward.[9]

To conclude, over the last two decades central banks have been forced to respond to two episodes of severe stress in global financial markets. This valuable hands-on experience should provide the basis for designing plans for future financial battles. While important progress has been made, more needs to be done. Momentum on outstanding reforms is slowing as the memory of the last crisis fades, while the need for careful planning has become more urgent given the increased speed with which bank runs and contagion can occur. The remainder of this book provides more concrete suggestions for exactly how to construct these plans while drawing on the principles outlined by Sun Tzu.

3 Heaven: The Inevitability of Powerful External Shocks

When Sun Tzu discusses the importance of laying plans in advance, he continually highlights that this involves accepting the underlying conditions and constraints around which you must operate. These conditions—what he terms the "heaven" and "earth"—are outside a leader's control and can single-handedly determine the outcome of the battle. A leader who plans ahead may be able to shape some of these constraints a priori (such as moving an army to establish the terrain of the battlefield, the focus of chapter 4), but many of these constraints are immutable and must be worked around—no matter how challenging.

> The art of war, then, is governed by five constant factors, to be taken into account in one's deliberations, when seeking to determine the conditions obtaining in the field. (Sun Tzu, *The Art of War*, Chapter 1, Principle 3)
>
> Heaven signifies night and day, cold and heat, times and seasons. (Sun Tzu, *The Art of War*, Chapter 1, Principle 7)
>
> These five heads should be familiar to every general: he who knows them will be victorious; he who knows them not will fail. (Sun Tzu, *The Art of War*, Chapter 1, Principle 11)

Some of these external constraints included in heaven are predictable (such as the hours of daylight) and therefore easier to plan around. In many cases, however, these external factors are hard to forecast and can suddenly materialize—such as extreme heat that saps the energy of the troops, a snowstorm that blocks a mountain crossing, or heavy rain that turns the battlefield into mud. The impact of these "heavenly" events can overwhelm carefully laid strategies and defeat a powerful army. For example, even the formidable armies of Napoleon and Hitler were emasculated by the cold Russian weather. Similarly, central banks should make plans that take into account the risk of extreme events and contagion from external shocks, even if more challenging to forecast than the weather.

This chapter discusses how external global shocks have become more important for monetary policy. In fact, during certain periods these heavenly shocks have been the dominant drivers of macroeconomic variables, thereby causing a high degree of synchronization in central bank decisions around the world (similar to how some heavenly events simultaneously affect both armies on a battlefield). The chapter discusses what drives these global shocks and how their role varies across countries and variables, before ending with suggestions for how central banks can better adapt given the unpredictability and power of these heavenly events. Even if central banks and generals cannot change the weather, there are ways to operate more effectively during storms as well as sunshine.

Shocks from Heaven: A Large and Growing Role

Global economic activity and inflation have been unusually volatile over the last two decades. Figures 3.1 and 3.2 show mean and median real GDP growth and CPI (consumer price index) inflation for twenty-four advanced economies from 1980 through 2025 (with expected values for 2024 and 2025).[1] The sharp collapses in output around the GFC and the pandemic are striking. Average GDP growth crashed from an average of +3.0 percent over 1980–2007 to –3.6 percent in 2009 and –4.3 percent in 2020. This was particularly painful in this set of advanced economies for which average GDP growth had not fallen below 1 percent in the previous two and a half decades. CPI inflation has also been unusually volatile—with average inflation bouncing from below targets in much of the 2010s to well above in the early 2020s. Not only did inflation exceed the 2 percent goal set by many central banks, but it also spiked to a sample median of 8.1 percent in 2022—the highest in about forty years.

What is also striking, however, is the extent to which these sharp swings in global activity and inflation were shared broadly around the world, particularly in the advanced economies that are the focus of this book. Figure 3.3 shows the share of advanced economies defined as being in a recession (with annual GDP growth <0 percent) or "stagnant" (with annual GDP growth between 0 percent and 1 percent).[2] Figure 3.4 shows the share of advanced economies with inflation defined as "too hot" (above 2.5

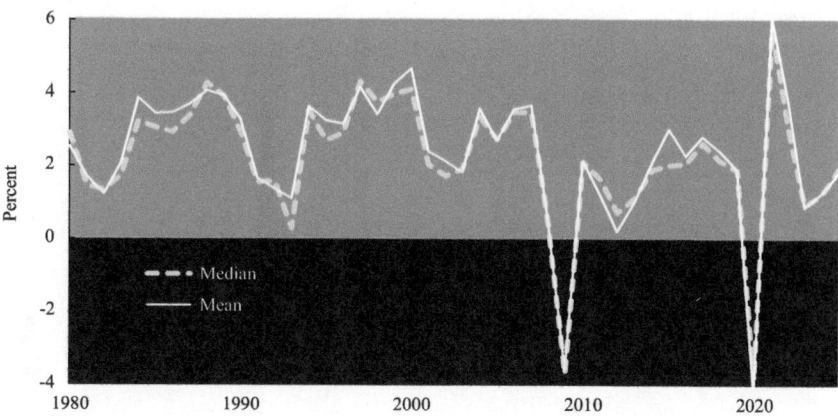

Figure 3.1
Real GDP growth in advanced economies: 1980–2025. *Note*: Sample is twenty-four advanced economies. GDP growth is annual real GDP growth from 1980 through 2025. Data for 2024 and 2025 are estimates. *Source*: Underlying data from the IMF's World Economic Outlook database (April 2024).

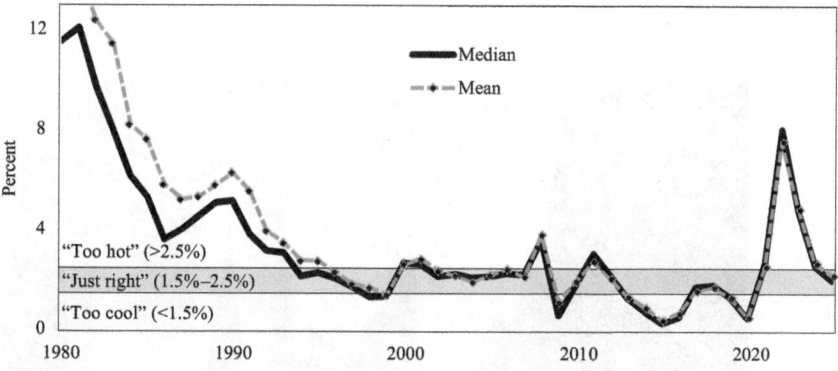

Figure 3.2
CPI inflation in advanced economies: 1980–2025. *Note*: Sample is twenty-four advanced economies. Inflation is average CPI inflation each year from 1980 through 2025, with estimates for 2024–2025. *Source*: Underlying data from the IMF's World Economic Outlook database (April 2024).

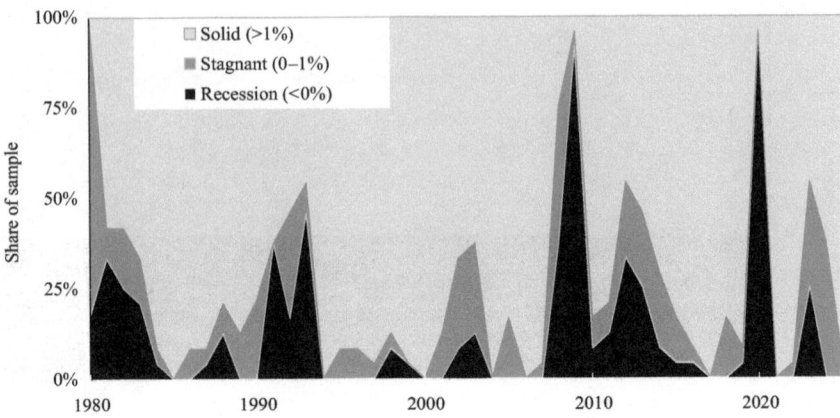

Figure 3.3
Distribution of GDP growth in advanced economies. *Note*: Share of sample of twenty-four advanced economies with annual real GDP growth at different thresholds. "Solid" growth is >1 percent. "Stagnant" growth is defined as 0–1 percent and "Recession" is defined as <0 percent. Data is from 1980 through 2025, with estimates for 2024–2025. *Source*: Underlying data from the IMF's World Economic Outlook database (April 2024).

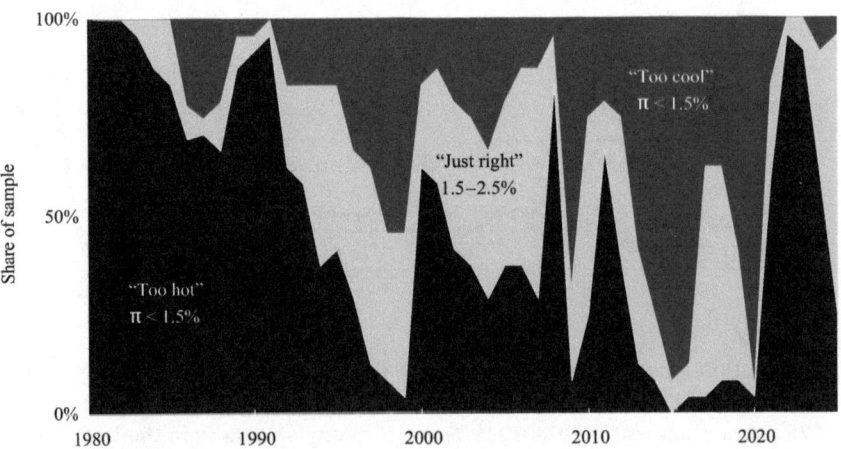

Figure 3.4
Distribution of CPI inflation in advanced economies. *Note*: Share of twenty-four advanced economies with average CPI inflation at each threshold per year. Data for 1980–2025, estimates for 2024–2025. *Source*: Underlying data from the IMF's World Economic Outlook database (April 2024).

percent), "too cool" (defined as below 1 percent), and "just right" (defined as from 1.5 percent to 2.5 percent). Each graph shows steep waves, periods when most economies experience swings in growth or inflation in the same direction. For example, almost all economies were in a recession around the GFC and the pandemic, and most economies had inflation that was "too cool" in 2015 and "too hot" in 2022. Granted, there are periods when different countries had different challenges, such as in 2003 when the sample was almost evenly split between those with inflation "too hot," "too cool," and "just right." But the last two decades are largely dominated by periods when economic activity and inflation are highly synchronized across a large portion of advanced economies.

What do these synchronized shifts in growth and inflation imply for central bank decisions? Figure 3.5 (from Forbes, Ha, and Kose 2024b) shows the share of central banks in advanced economies that tightened monetary policy (through raising policy interest rates) or eased monetary policy

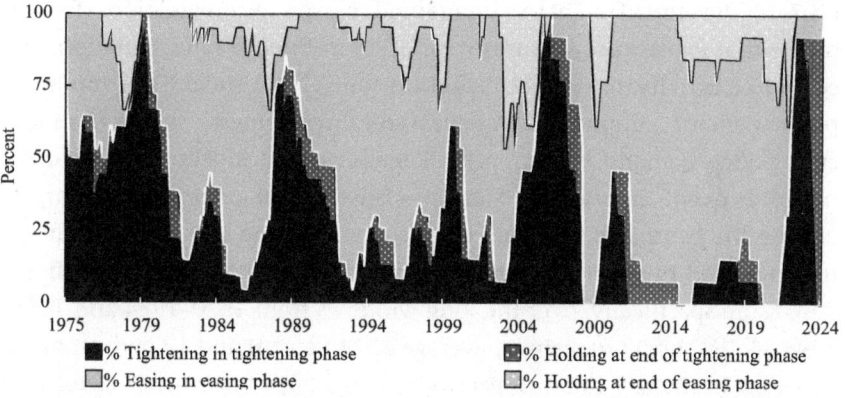

Figure 3.5

Share of advanced economies in tightening and easing phases. *Note*: Share of economies each month that are tightening monetary policy by raising interest rates or easing monetary policy by reducing interest rates or doing quantitative easing (QE), based on the definitions of tightening and easing phases in Forbes, Ha, and Kose (2024b). Holding is defined as the period after any adjustments in interest rates and after the end of any QE programs before a central bank shifts to the opposite phase (i.e., either tightening or easing). Sample includes twenty-four advanced economies from January 1975 through May 2024, with phases for individual Euro area countries through 1998 and then for the European Central Bank (ECB) from 1999 through 2024. *Source*: Replicated from chart 19 in Forbes, Ha, and Kose (2024b).

(through lowering policy interest rates or asset purchase programs) since 1975.[3] The lighter shades of each color denote the share of economies with monetary policy "on hold" at the end of each tightening and easing phase. There is a high degree of synchronization in how central banks adjust monetary policy. All economies were easing monetary policy during the 2008 and 2020 recessions, and most when inflation was "too cool" in the 2010s. During the post-pandemic period when inflation was "too hot," most economies were actively tightening monetary policy.[4] Moreover, central banks often suddenly shift their policies all at the same time—causing the steep slopes to the mountains in the figure. This high degree of comovement in central bank decisions during certain periods is not surprising; it is a natural response to sharp, synchronized movements in the key variables (growth and inflation) that affect monetary policy.

An even more interesting question is: What drives these synchronized movements in growth, inflation, and the corresponding adjustments in interest rates? To better understand these patterns, Forbes, Ha, and Kose (2024b) developed a factor-augmented vector autoregression (FAVAR) model that explains the monthly variation in interest rates, inflation, and economic activity since 1970 based on four global shocks (for monetary policy, demand, supply, and oil prices) and three domestic shocks (for monetary policy, demand, and supply).[5] The four global shocks are comparable to the "heaven" discussed by Sun Tzu—the external factors that are largely outside the control of any individual economy.[6] The role of global shocks has increased over time—particularly for interest rates (left side of figure 3.6). More specifically, over the long windows from 1970–1984 and 1985–1998, global shocks explain an average of 24 percent and 19 percent of the variation in interest rates, respectively. This jumps to about 38 percent of the variation over the 1999–2019 period, and then increases even further to 49 percent over 2020–2023. In other words, about half of the variation in interest rates from 2020 to 2023 was driven by global shocks.

The role of these global shocks has also been increasing over time for inflation and growth.[7] More specifically, the average role of global shocks driving inflation increases from 18 percent over 1985–1998 to 39 percent in 2020–2023, and for growth increases from 23 percent to 40 percent over the same windows. It is noteworthy that the role of global factors in explaining the variation in interest rates increases even more than that for the other macroeconomic variables on which monetary policy is based. Central banks appear to be driven more and more by heavenly events outside their control.

To better understand exactly what is driving these heavenly events, the right side of figure 3.6 shows a more detailed decomposition into seven shocks (from Forbes, Ha, and Kose 2024a,b). The role of global supply shocks (including from oil prices) has increased over time—with a larger role for these global supply shocks over 2020–2023 than during any historical precedent (including the major oil shocks and corresponding sharp increases in interest rates in the 1970s and 1980s). Global demand shocks, however, can also be important—and even more important for some macroeconomic variables. For example, global demand shocks explain a larger share of the variation in interest rates over 2020–2023 than global supply shocks (including oil prices). In contrast, the impact of global supply shocks is greater for inflation and growth than that of global demand shocks. This is consistent with monetary policy responding more to demand than supply shocks—the optimal strategy in most circumstances.[8]

The role of these shocks can also vary meaningfully across countries—and differ from the averages reported previously in important ways. Figure 3.7 shows the same decompositions over 2020–2023 for each of the individual economies used to construct the averages in figure 3.6. There are a number of noteworthy patterns, such as the outsized role of oil and other global supply shocks in driving the variation in interest rates and inflation in the Euro area. Switzerland also stands out for monetary policy being particularly vulnerable to global shocks, with 87 percent of its variation in interest rates explained by global factors (the largest after the Euro area). For Switzerland, however, the role of these global shocks is relatively more muted for inflation and growth (at 37 percent and 24 percent, respectively). This is the reverse of the case in most other advanced economies, for which global shocks play a relatively greater role for inflation and growth than for interest rates. This likely reflects the outsized role Switzerland plays in financial markets and as a safe-haven currency, such that monetary policy is relatively more sensitive to global shocks than the other macroeconomic variables.

Although the role of global shocks varies across countries and macroeconomic variables, the overall trend is clear: over the last two decades, global shocks have played a growing and, in some cases, dominant role in driving key measures of macroeconomic activity and the corresponding responses

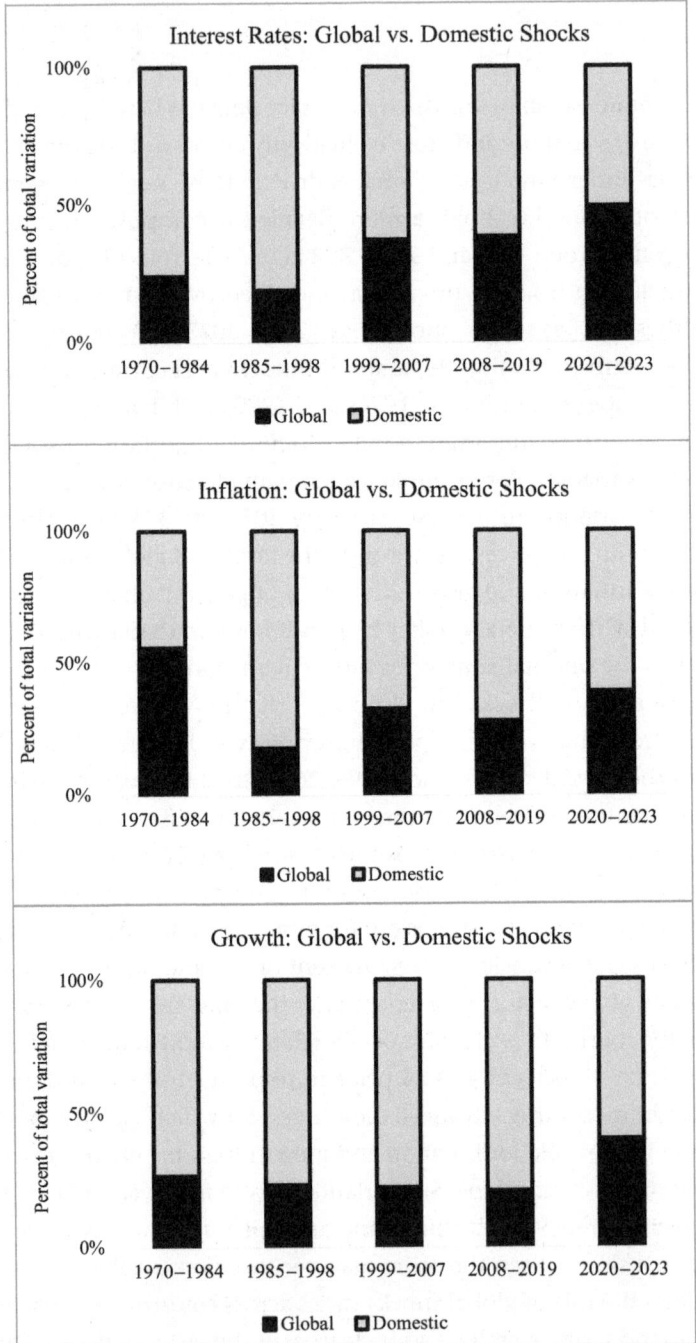

Figure 3.6
Average contributions of shocks to interest rates, inflation, and output growth. *Note*: Figures show percent of variation in monthly interest rates, inflation, or output growth driven by shocks listed at bottom based on a FAVAR model with seven shocks. Interest rates are measured using the shadow interest rate, and if not

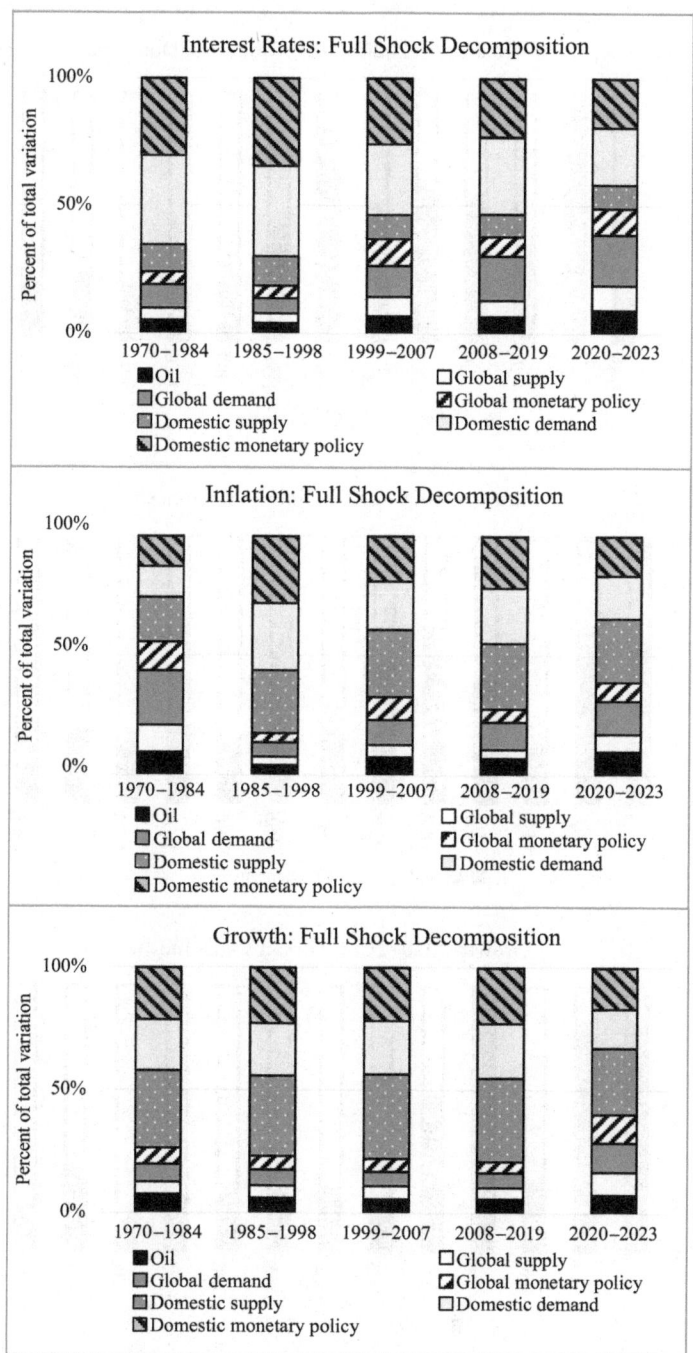

available, the overnight rate or three-month yield. Inflation is average CPI inflation and output growth is the growth in industrial production. Results are averages for the thirteen advanced economies reported in figure 3.7. *Source*: Based on data and methodology from Forbes, Ha, and Kose (2024b), but extends sample from five to thirteen advanced economies.

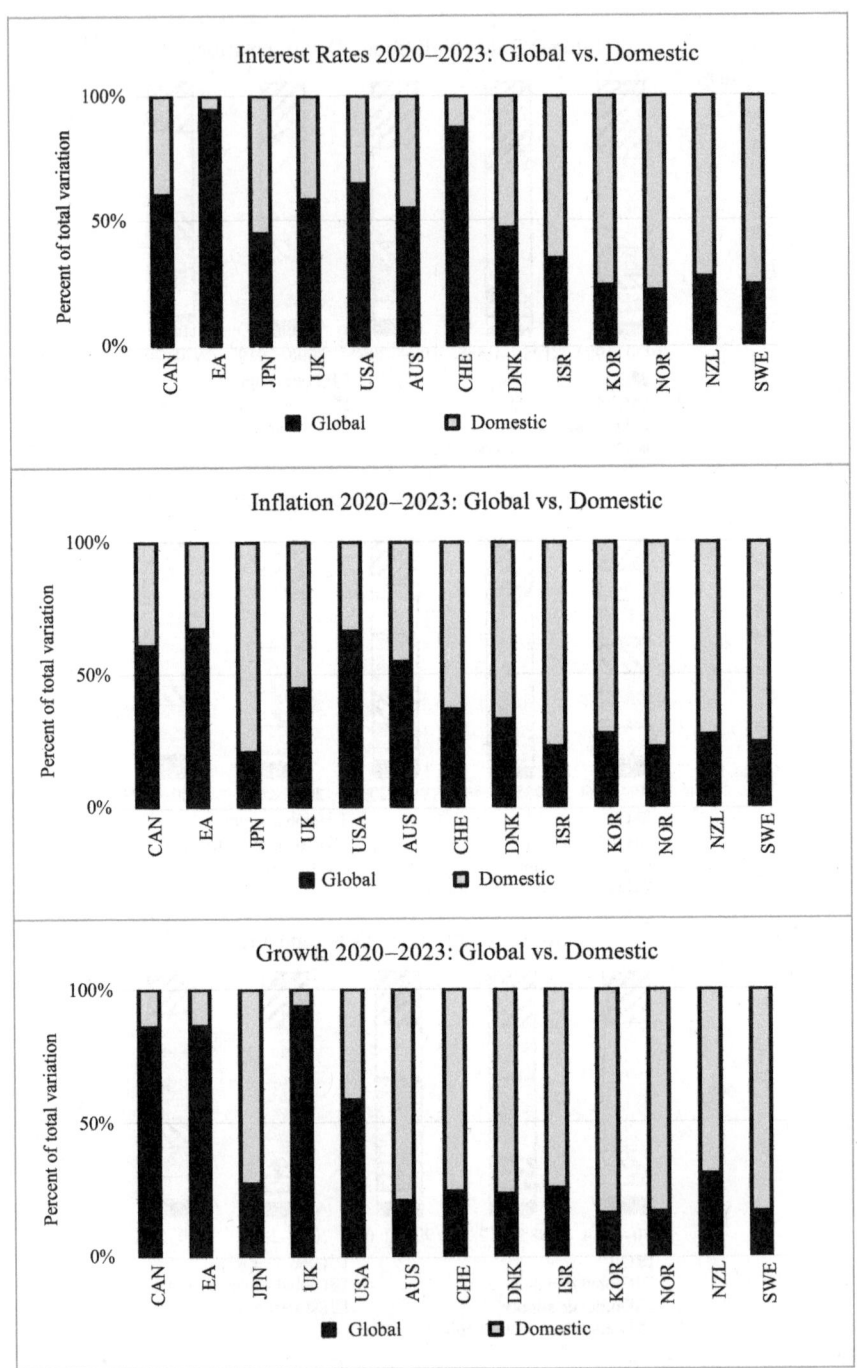

Figure 3.7
Contributions of shocks: organized by economy. *Note*: See note to figure 3.6 for details on data and estimation. Countries included are Canada (CAN), Euro area (EA), Japan (JPN), United Kingdom (UK), United States (USA), Australia (AUS), Switzerland

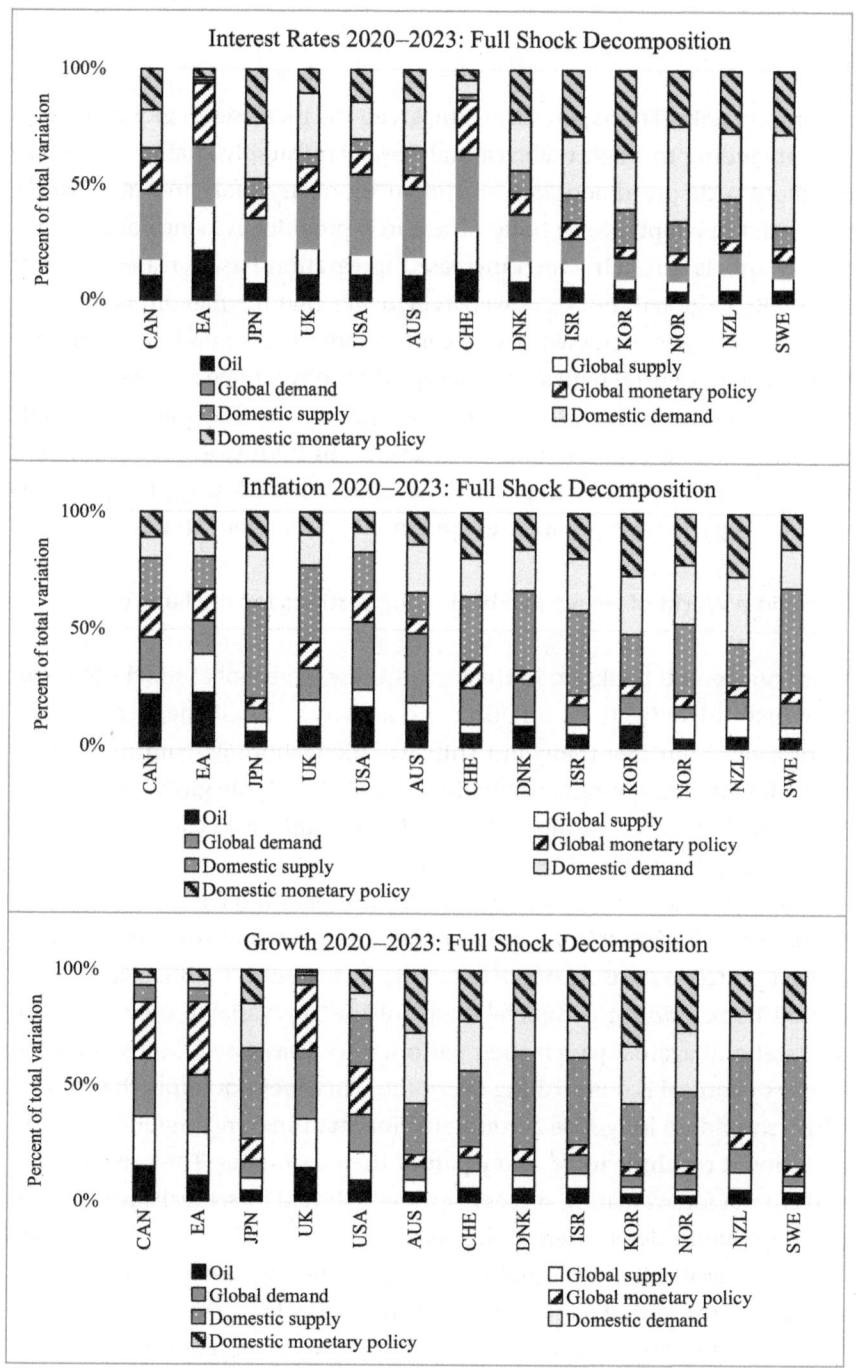

(CHE), Denmark (DNK), Israel (ISR), South Korea (KOR), Norway (NOR), New Zealand (NZL) and Sweden (SWE). *Source*: Based on data and methodology from Forbes, Ha, and Kose (2024b), but extends sample from five to thirteen advanced economies.

of central banks. This is not surprising given the increases in global integration (including through trade, capital flows, and supply chains), as well as the more widespread adoption of similar monetary tools and frameworks (discussed in chapter 5). A body of research provides evidence of the multiple channels through which increased integration has increased country sensitivity to global shocks, as well as evidence that the magnitude of these global shocks has increased over recent decades (particularly in commodity markets).[9] Central banks must accept that they will be affected by these external events outside of their control—just as Sun Tzu warned generals that they must accept the role of "heaven." In both cases, these external shocks can be impossible to predict and undermine existing plans, but it is still necessary to incorporate these potential risks in your strategies.

Living in a World of Heavenly Shocks: Suggestions for the Future

What can central banks do in the face of these large global shocks that can have first-order effects on inflation and activity? Even if the recent movement away from free trade and shift to "friendshoring" continues, most countries are likely to remain highly integrated with the global economy.[10] There are, however, a number of steps that central banks can take to better adapt to this large role of heaven.

First, countries must accept that external shocks will continue to play an outsized role in determining inflation rates, thereby limiting their ability to achieve a precise measure of price stability at any point in time. Put bluntly, central banks cannot completely control the key variable they are asked to target and against which their performance is assessed. Moreover, their degree of control is diminishing over time. This does not imply that central banks should no longer be accountable for attaining price stability; that is, and should continue to be, a key part of their mandates. The specific goals and criteria for evaluating success, however, should be set realistically given this dominant role of external shocks.

More specifically, this could involve modifying the inflation targets established for central banks, such that they allow for more short-term variation resulting from heavenly shocks. For example, inflation targets could be set based on a measure of underlying inflation that is less sensitive to energy and food prices (such as core inflation, albeit the specifics would vary by country). Or the inflation target could involve inflation being on track to reach a target in a fixed amount of time (say two or three years) rather than each month, so that the impact of temporary, external shocks would have dissipated. These more realistic targets are already used in some economies—such as Bank of England and Swiss National Bank (which target inflation in two or three years, respectively) and the Federal Reserve (which often focuses on recent developments in core inflation instead of headline inflation, although the official target is the latter).

Granted, most central banks currently ignore short-lived volatility in headline inflation rates, so that officially shifting the target to underlying inflation or where inflation is forecast in two to three years is already de facto being implemented in many cases. Nonetheless, this explicit change in targets would improve communication and lead to a more productive evaluation of central bank actions. For example, a common "straw man" argument heard in 2024 is that central banks should not be blamed for the sharp increase in the price level over 2021–2023 as raising rates to keep inflation at 2 percent over this period would have caused an extreme recession. That is not a useful comparison. A better metric would be evaluating whether central banks made the optimal rate decisions to steer inflation toward their targets within two to three years and after the impact of the large supply shocks had faded.

Closely related, another approach could involve setting a band or range for the inflation target—rather than focusing on a precise number down to one decimal point (such as 2.0 percent).[11] Global shocks will constantly cause inflation to veer from a forecast, even in fairly stable times when the role of external shocks is more muted. Central banks should not feel pressure to respond to each small, external fluctuation that could soon reverse. Attempting to achieve a precise target could generate excess volatility in interest rates, creating unnecessary challenges for households and businesses. Moreover, in some situations inflation may deviate from a precise target for an extended period (such as inflation settling at 1.9 percent or 2.1 percent), and if the Phillips curve (the correlation between unemployment and inflation) is flat, reaching 2.0 percent could require large adjustments in interest rates, economic activity, and unemployment. The cost of closing the small gap relative to a precise inflation target could exceed any benefits. Changing inflation targets to bands (including a framework such as the SNB's target of keeping inflation at or below 2 percent) would provide central banks with more flexibility to evaluate the overall costs and benefits of adjusting monetary policy for the broader economy, without worrying about the implications of small deviations from an overly precise target.

A second set of recommendations for central banks in this world of large external shocks is to better incorporate these global shocks in their models and inflation forecasts. Granted, some central banks (particularly small open economies that are more sensitive to exchange rate fluctuations and commodity-exporting economies that are more sensitive to commodity price fluctuations) already do put substantial weight on global developments in their models and discussions. I am continually surprised, however, at how other large economies have been slower to incorporate the risks around potent external shocks. For example, many prominent models of U.S. inflation dynamics still continue to place minimal emphasis on global factors. A popular strategy is to control for domestic variables (domestic slack, inflation expectations, and often lagged inflation) plus include one control for import prices, which is perceived to be a sufficient statistic to capture any effects of the global economy on domestic inflation.[12] Simply replacing the single, rough proxy for global factors with more explicit controls for global factors (such as oil prices, other commodity prices, supply chains, and the exchange rate) can meaningfully improve a simple model's ability to explain and forecast inflation (Forbes 2020). This improvement from including more specific controls for global factors in models has grown over time—as expected given the growing role for global shocks.

A third, and closely related, recommendation is to better differentiate between the types of global shocks incorporated in central bank models (as also argued in Forbes, Ha, and Kose 2024a,b). There is a tendency to view global shocks as primarily supply shocks. This is not surprising; many supply shocks receive substantial media attention—such as a pandemic shutting down international supply chains, a large ship blocking the Suez Canal, or a military conflict involving a commodity exporter. Yet global demand shocks are often more important than global supply shocks (although the relative roles vary across countries, the variable being explained, and time periods), as shown in figures 3.6 and 3.7.

Moreover, since supply shocks usually merit a more muted monetary policy response than demand shocks, correctly identifying the source of the global shock is critical for central banks.[13] An overestimation of the role of global supply shocks may have occurred over 2020–2023 (which is not surprising given the prominent and headline-grabbing supply shocks around COVID-19 and Russia's invasion of Ukraine), and this likely contributed to the slow pivot to tightening monetary policy in response to the postpandemic inflation (as discussed in chapter 6). Granted, identifying global supply and demand shocks in real time is challenging, especially during periods of heightened macroeconomic volatility. Improving our ability to accurately identify the sources of these global shocks will be increasingly crucial, however, as international factors are likely to continue to play an outsized role in the determinants of interest rates and inflation.

A final suggestion for central banks in today's world of large external shocks is to make better use of scenarios or alternate forecasting techniques to better prepare businesses, households, and governments for the volatility that could occur from specific heavenly events. Most central banks currently focus on a baseline scenario with a central case for how the economy is expected to evolve. This baseline is usually surrounded by large error bands showing the imprecision of the estimates, but the error bands are so wide and capture so many unexplained tweaks in the model that they are largely ignored. Central banks could also present several concrete, alternate scenarios (in addition to the baseline), including scenarios that reflect the impact of specific global shocks (such as an escalation of violence in a country that is central to supply chains or oil prices, or both). Central banks could then provide clear guidance on how inflation and interest rates could veer from the baseline in response to these specific global shocks. By clearly laying out these scenarios, businesses, households, and financial institutions would hopefully be more likely to prepare for these eventualities (such as financial institutions hedging the risks and households more carefully assessing whether to pay a premium for a fixed mortgage rate).

To conclude, Sun Tzu's warnings of the role of heaven apply to central bankers of all religions around the world. External shocks—beyond the control of any army or central bank—are a fact of life. For central banks, the role of these global shocks has been growing over time and recently been a dominant factor in monetary policy decisions. Even though there is little that can be done to alter what descends from heaven, there are several ways central banks can better prepare, adapt, and at least partially mitigate the subsequent disruptions.

4 Earth and Terrain: Establishing a Strong Tactical Position

When Sun Tzu highlights the critical importance of external conditions in determining success, he is also careful to distinguish between those emanating from "heaven" and from "earth." While careful planning cannot alter events originating in heaven, advance preparation can affect the constraints originating from earth (such as establishing a strong defensive position and avoiding being trapped in dangerous "terrain"). Once this tactical position is established, however, the resulting constraints from earth become as immutable as those from heaven.

> If you know Heaven and know Earth, you may make your victory complete. (Sun Tzu, *The Art of War*, Chapter 10, Principle 31)

> Earth comprises distances, great and small; danger and security; open ground and narrow passes; the chances of life and death. (Sun Tzu, *The Art of War*, Chapter 1, Principle 8)

> Security against defeat implies defensive tactics. . . . The general who is skilled in defense hides in the most secret recesses of the earth . . . thus . . . we have ability to protect ourselves. (Sun Tzu, *The Art of War*, Chapter 4, Principles 5 and 7)

Given the importance of these earthly conditions—combined with the ability of a leader to influence how these constraints bind—Sun Tzu spends an extensive amount of time explaining how to evaluate options and plan accordingly. For example, he describes nine varieties of ground (dispersive, facile, contentious, open, intersecting highways, serious, difficult, hemmed-in, desperate) and six types of terrain (ranging from accessible/"freely traversed" to entangling/"can be abandoned but is hard to reoccupy").[1] He devotes many pages to how this advance positioning determines the army's resilience and the options available once the battle begins. A strong tactical position can give troops a significant advantage in the subsequent battle—or leave no options but to fight to the death.

Similarly, central banks have some ability to establish the strength and resilience of their financial systems and economy before a crisis begins. A country with a strong macroprudential framework for the broader financial system, combined with strong prudential oversight of individual institutions, will start from a stronger defensive position against a range of shocks. In fact, this is one of the most important lessons learned over the last two decades. A lack of attention to macroprudential risks contributed to the severity of the GFC, while steps taken to strengthen macroprudential frameworks in the subsequent decade contributed to the greater resilience of the banking system during the pandemic. The technical details of this tactical position matter, however, just as they do in establishing the terrain for a military encounter. This chapter discusses how countries have improved their macroprudential terrain over the last two decades and what additional defenses should be built in order to ensure even more resilient positions in the future.[2]

The Importance of Establishing a Strong Tactical Position

One of the critically important lessons from the GFC was the importance of understanding and addressing macroprudential risks, particularly resulting from interconnected financial institutions.[3] With the benefit of hindsight, it is surprising how little attention had been paid to these fragilities, especially in advanced economies. The dangers of this shaky ground became apparent in 2008 when weakness in one sector (U.S. housing) spread not only around the world, but also to small banks, to larger investment banks, to insurance companies, and then money market funds. This experience was a poignant lesson that vulnerabilities in the financial system can amplify an economic shock and turn a moderate recession into the most severe collapse in the global economy since the Great Depression.

This experience spurred a major rethink of how to design comprehensive macroprudential frameworks to mitigate these risks and amplification effects in the future. There has been meaningful progress.[4] International institutions, central banks, and other policy groups launched major initiatives to study and address macrofinancial vulnerabilities (FSF 2009; CGFS 2010; IMF 2014a; ESRB 2021a,b). These discussions prioritized three related objectives: addressing excessive credit expansion and strengthening resilience in the overall financial system; reducing key amplification mechanisms of systemic risk; and mitigating structural vulnerabilities related to the role of important institutions in key markets. To address these priorities, a range of tools and instruments have been developed around capital/reserves, liquidity, credit risk, and the resolution of systemically important institutions (Claessens 2015; CGFS 2012; IMF 2014a,b).

As these approaches and tools were developed, many countries established new macroprudential authorities to oversee this work and then implement a combination of the new instruments that made sense given each economy's characteristics and vulnerabilities. There has been substantial progress since the GFC. For example, figure 4.1 shows one measure of aggregate changes in macroprudential policy since 1990 across 134 economies.[5] There were minimal adjustments in the 1990s, and only modest use of these tools (mainly in emerging markets) during the 2000s. As a result, on the eve of the GFC, macroprudential policy had only been tightened fewer than two times per country (on net, averaged across economies) over the previous eighteen years. After 2010, however, countries began to

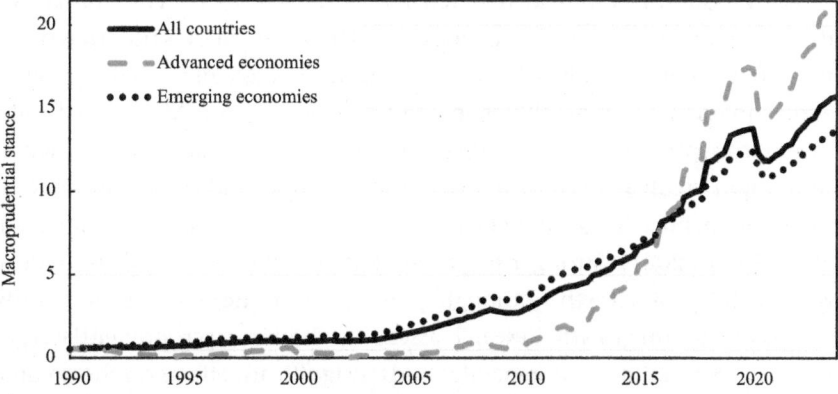

Figure 4.1
Average macroprudential stance by country group over time. *Note*: Graph shows the average annual macroprudential stance for each group of countries. The stance is calculated as the net changes in macroprudential policy each year (with a +1 for a tightening of any macroprudential policy and a −1 for each loosening), and then the changes are cumulated each year starting in 1990 (which is set at 0). See Bergant and Forbes (2023a) and Forbes (2019) for details. *Source*: Based on data from the IMF's Integrated Macroprudential Policy (iMaPP) database, described in Alam et al. (2019), with data available as of January 22, 2025. Country classification based on IMF's World Economic Outlook database.

tighten macroprudential policy more frequently, so that by 2016 the average net macroprudential stance was five tightenings and by the end of the sample in October 2023 there were over fifteen tightenings.

An important component of this new set of macroprudential tools is assessing the potential risks from severe financial stress in major financial institutions (an example of the planning ahead recommended in chapter 2). More specially, many economies now require that systemically important financial institutions (SIFIs) develop resolution plans (i.e., "living wills") detailing in advance how they would be wound down in the event of material financial distress or failure. Many central banks also employ regular stress tests assessing how financial institutions would be affected in different scenarios. This allows regulators to better understand their vulnerabilities and risks, with the goal of not only identifying, but also mitigating any weakness in advance. Most economies have also significantly tightened capital and liquidity requirements for all regulated institutions in order to build stronger defenses against a range of shocks.

As countries used these macroprudential tools more actively, a rapidly growing body of empirical research has been able to provide initial evidence of what works—and what does not.[6] This assessment is not straightforward, but generally finds that these reforms have made meaningful progress addressing some vulnerabilities in the financial system.[7] More specifically, macroprudential policy can mitigate specific exposures of concern (such as from rapid credit growth or foreign exchange risk) and provide somewhat more independence for monetary policy (Araujo et al. 2020; Bergant et al. 2020; Forbes 2021). Stronger macroprudential regulations may also reduce the volatility of growth, although potentially at the expense of slightly slower short-term growth. Research assessing whether macroprudential regulations affect capital flows generally finds insignificant effects on the volume of flows, but some impact on the composition of flows (i.e., duration and type of capital flow).[8]

Although macroprudential regulations have strengthened the defenses of banking systems, they also have unintended consequences that can, in turn, generate other vulnerabilities. Tightening macroprudential policy generates spillovers and leakages as financial intermediation shifts outside the regulated banking sector to non-bank financial institutions (NBFIs), also referred to as the "shadow" financial system, including corporate bond markets, mutual funds, hedge funds, money market funds, venture capital, insurance companies, real estate investment trusts, and housing finance (Ahnert et al. 2021; Avdjiev et al. 2017; Forbes 2019). For example, when tighter regulations reduce lending by domestic banks, lending increases through NBFIs and foreign banks, muting the overall impact on credit growth.[9] Granted, the increased lending by NBFIs and international banks only partially compensates for the reduction in credit from domestic banks, but it is unclear how these shifts in financial intermediation effect the resilience of the system overall.[10] NBFIs are generally less regulated than banks (albeit with substantial variation across countries and industries), so that central banks are less likely to understand the fragilities that emerge as more financial intermediation shifts away from banks. NBFIs can also be less hedged and less prepared for financial shocks, leading to greater volatility and a risk their actions could amplify shocks across the broader financial system in ways that are hard to predict.

The pandemic provided an initial (albeit very extreme) test of how this greater use of macroprudential regulations (and the corresponding leakages), has affected the resilience of financial systems. The preliminary assessment is promising, even if also identifying vulnerabilities that still need to be addressed. Starting with the good news, countries that had tightened macroprudential regulations by more before the pandemic generally experienced less financial and economic stress during the period of market turmoil in the spring of 2020 (Bergant and Forbes 2023a). Moreover, countries that had tightened regulations by more before the pandemic were subsequently able to ease them by more when the pandemic hit and thereby provide more support for financial markets, credit availability, and broader economic growth. Although these results are just correlations during a tumultuous period that makes it hard to identify the impact of any one policy, macroprudential tools were used actively and in a way that should support resilience.

The experience, however, also provided a warning of how NBFIs have become more vulnerable to financial shocks, and that banks may have meaningful exposure to this sector in a way that could propagate stress in the future. For example, in countries that had tightened macroprudential regulations more aggressively, bond and equity portfolio investors amplified risk shocks (increasing outflows by more during "risk off" episodes and increasing inflows by more during "risk on" episodes) in a large and economically meaningful way (Chari, Dilts-Stedman, and Forbes 2022). Also, banks more exposed to this shadow financial system were significantly

more vulnerable during the period of stress around the pandemic, suggesting they are more interlinked with NBFIs than generally appreciated
(Forbes, Friedrich, and Reinhardt 2023).[11] This suggests that if central
banks and governments had not provided substantial liquidity and market
support benefiting a broad range of financial institutions in response to
response crises, banks might not have been as fortified as suggested by the
stronger capital and liquidity positions. As banks and NBFIs adjust to the
new regulatory environment, they are changing their business models in
ways that may make them more interrelated—and more vulnerable in different ways—than in the past (Acharya, Carletti, et al. 2024).

To summarize, macroprudential regulations have meaningfully strengthened the defensive position of banks, but may have generated more vulnerable terrain in other parts of the financial system. There is more work to be
done.

Improving Tactical Positions: Suggestions for the Future

What more can be done to strengthen the terrain on which the financial system rests? Central banks should address the vulnerabilities that we already
know exist (particularly those around the shifts in financial intermediation
to NBFIs as discussed earlier), as well as think more creatively about new
"battle" scenarios and the institutional structures to best support strong
defenses in the future.

A first step is to more aggressively address the vulnerabilities that have
already emerged in the shadow financial system. Financial regulators are
already aware of many of these risks (FSB 2024a; ESRB 2021a, 2024), but
reform momentum has slowed as economies have recovered, memories of
the last crisis fade, and financial institutions lobby against additional (often
costly) regulations. The crisis in the UK pension industry in September 2022—
when problems in the relatively small sector of liability-driven investing
(LDI) quickly spread to the heart of the large UK government bond market
should be a wake-up call. Central banks and regulators need to continue to
make progress identifying these types of risks in NBFIs and strengthening
their tactical positions. In cases where the risks in these institutions cannot
be sufficiently addressed, central banks should prioritize developing plans
to provide liquidity or market support in emergencies to avoid stress in
this sector from undermining the broader financial system (as discussed in

chapter 2). Ongoing work in several international financial groups, such as the Financial Stability Board and the European Systemic Risk Board, provides a useful set of priorities for this next set of reforms.

As a second and closely related step, this next phase of reforms should also focus on better understanding the exposure of banks to the shadow financial system. There is a popular narrative that banks have sufficiently strengthened their defensive positions and are now "fixed," as they were largely resilient during the period of heightened market stress in the spring of 2020. Central banks, however, provided substantial market and liquidity support during this period (see chapter 5), much of which benefited NBFIs. Given the continued linkages between banks and NBFIs, it is unclear if banks would have appeared so resilient without this general support.

Third, regulators should make greater use of cyclical macroprudential regulations. While calibrating the appropriate level of these regulations is not straightforward, these countercyclical measures could be used more effectively to moderate swings in the financial cycle and temper the economy during both booms and busts. This involves raising buffers during periods of credit expansion to moderate overheating and the buildup of financial vulnerabilities, as well as quickly reducing buffers during periods of stress to mitigate any contraction in credit and the corresponding deleveraging. Research shows that these buffers should be adjusted by much larger increments than they have been to date—and particularly tightened more during recoveries.[12]

A fourth suggestion for central banks to further strengthen their tactical positioning is to be more creative in their hypothetical scenarios of the next battle. Many of the "stress tests" currently draw from the battle (such as vulnerabilities in mortgage markets). These are important, but the next crisis is more likely to start in other sectors which have not been fortified. Additional stress tests and scenario analysis should logically begin with preidentified areas of weakness—such as commercial real estate today—but central banks should also not shy away from modelling low probability but high risk events (such as a global pandemic). This could include modelling events that are politically sensitive, such as a military attack on a region critical to supply chains, or a spike in borrowing spreads linked to some type of fiscal news. This should also involve learning from vulnerabilities that were previously missed. For example, why did the regulators who examined the UK pension industry miss how stress in this sector could trigger a collapse in the broader UK gilt market in 2022? Even if institutions appear to be well hedged (as was the UK pension industry), what types of scenarios could trigger stress that is amplified across the financial system? Even if this type of analysis cannot predict exactly how the next crisis unwinds, it could go some way in identifying the types of vulnerabilities that could become a problem, forcing central banks to think creatively about how they would respond. Drafting a range of responses to very different scenarios should provide useful blueprints to quickly draw from in a crisis (particularly as there may be minimal time to respond, as discussed in chapter 2).

A final suggestion for fortifying an economy's defensive position is to strengthen the institutions implementing macroprudential policy (including as part of the discussion to improve planning and trade-offs in chapters 2 and 7, respectively). Although many countries have some type of committee or institution in charge of macroprudential regulations, oversight of different types of NBFIs can be diffuse and not well coordinated (particularly in the United States). Most central banks have adjusted countercyclical regulations slowly and by less than models suggest is optimal, and some vulnerabilities that previously emerged are still not addressed (as discussed earlier). This is not surprising. Tightening macroprudential regulations can be politically challenging, as the costs in terms of reduced access to credit are immediate and apparent, while the benefits are more amorphous and may not appear for years. The optimal macroprudential authority should have some independence and be insulated from the political cycle, while at the same time maintaining a high degree of transparency and accountability, as macroprudential regulations can affect consumers, firms, and the broader economy. Several frameworks show promise, such as the Financial Policy Committee at the Bank of England, which includes a range of expertise and external members that must show their independence through regular testimony before a government committee.

All in all, although financial systems have been fortified meaningfully over the last two decades, there is still more that could be done to bolster their defenses and ensure they are on a terrain that provides the strongest tactical position for the next financial battle.

5 Maneuvering: Combining Weapons and Methods

While Sun Tzu begins *The Art of War* by discussing the constraints from "heaven" and "earth," he allocates even more space to the many variables that leaders can control and influence through their decisions. A key focus is how to maneuver and choose the optimal combination of methods—including both traditional weapons and other "indirect" strategies. When deciding whether to employ an individual tool or tactic, a leader must consider whether it is appropriate for the given challenge, as well as how it interacts with other strategies in use.

> In all fighting, the direct method may be used for joining battle, but the indirect methods will be needed in order to secure victory. (Sun Tzu, *The Art of War*, Chapter 5, Principle 5)

> In battle, there are not more than two methods of attack—the direct and the indirect; yet these two in combination give rise to an endless series of maneuvers. (Sun Tzu, *The Art of War*, Chapter 5, Principle 10)

> Water shapes its course according to the nature of the ground over which it flows; the soldier works out his victory in relation to the foe whom he is facing. (Sun Tzu, *The Art of War*, Chapter 6, Principle 28)

Over the centuries, central banks have used many combinations of methods to achieve price stability. For example, in the early 1800s the Bank of England (BoE) consulted a weathervane as an indicator of how to adjust the money supply, as it affected how many ships could sail up the Thames to unload cargo (thereby affecting economic activity).[1] This tool is still proudly displayed in the BoE's formal Court Room, even if it is no longer used to shape monetary policy. In the late 1970s and early 1980s, a number of countries focused on the growth in monetary aggregates,[2] while in the 1980s and 1990s many European countries relied partly on pegging their exchange rates under the European Monetary System. In 1990, the Reserve Bank of New Zealand officially adopted inflation targeting—a framework that has since spread to most advanced economies (and many emerging markets) around the world.

Over the last two decades, the severity of the economic and financial crises around the GFC and the pandemic forced central banks to innovate and rapidly develop a multifaceted set of new tools.[3] The most prominent weapons in this new armory were programs in which central banks purchased assets or provided liquidity and market support, or both. This chapter explores what central banks have learned about combining the "conventional" tool of adjusting policy interest rates with the "unconventional" tools of quantitative easing (QE), quantitative tightening (QT), and other balance sheet programs—similar to the strategies for combining the "direct" and "indirect" methods discussed by Sun Tzu. The chapter begins by examining their aggressive use in response to recent downturns and financial crises, and then their more hesitant use during the post-pandemic recovery and spike in inflation. It concludes with lessons from this experience over the last two decades on the symmetries and asymmetries in the use of and interaction between these tools, as well as suggestions to better combine various tactics in the future. The next chapter addresses the closely related issue of how using multiple tools simultaneously can restrict a central bank's flexibility to maneuver.

Maneuvering During Downturns and Crises

Central banks have been remarkably resourceful at responding to the two major battles of the last two decades: the GFC and the pandemic. Beginning in 2008, when it became clear that economic activity would slow sharply, central banks responded with their traditional first line of defense: reducing policy interest rates (shown in figure 5.1 for eight major advanced economies). This is the standard monetary policy response to support investment, consumption, employment, and growth. As the extent of the crisis became apparent, however, it was clear that more firepower would be needed.

The new weapons involved a variety of programs aimed at ensuring financial markets continued to function and solvent financial institutions could access liquidity. This did not, however, mean supporting prices at a certain level or avoiding all bankruptcies. To accomplish this, central

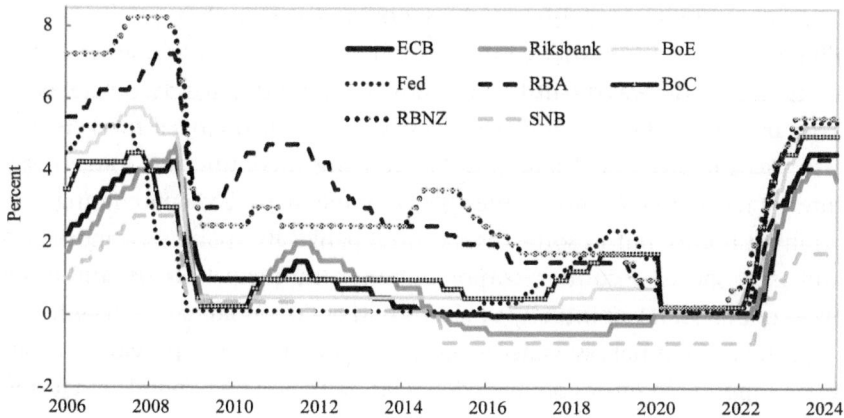

Figure 5.1

Policy interest rates in advanced economies. *Note*: Policy interest rates in percent for
each central bank. Data is from January 2006 through May 2024. Central banks are
ECB (European Central Bank), Fed (U.S. Federal Reserve), RBNZ (Reserve Bank of New
Zealand), Riksbank (Swedish Riksbank), RBA (Reserve Bank of Australia), SNB (Swiss
National Bank), BoE (Bank of England), and BoC (Bank of Canada). *Source*: Underly-
ing data from Bank for International Settlements, Haver Analytics, and OECD.

banks often worked in conjunction with national Treasury Departments
(or Finance Ministries) to introduce a range of liquidity programs aimed
at keeping financial institutions open and supporting the flow of credit
to consumers and businesses, as well as guarantee programs aimed at supporting critical funding markets for financial institutions. In some cases,
this also involved recapitalization to prevent the collapse of major financial
institutions that were believed to have systemic implications.[4]

A few examples from just the Federal Reserve's early response to the GFC
exhibit this range of new tactics.[5] It introduced the Term Auction Facility
(TAF) in December 2007 to provide liquidity to financially sound institutions
while attempting to avoid the stigma linked to other facilities by auctioning
short-term loans to depository institutions. Then it launched the Term Securities Lending Facility (TSLF) in March 2008, to provide access to collateral
and term funding to primary dealers, and the Primary Dealer Credit Facility
(PDCF), to help primary dealers provide overnight financing to securities
market participants. When strains appeared in currency markets, particularly in obtaining access to dollars, the Federal Reserve introduced and then
expanded a series of central bank swap lines with select countries.

A key component of this initial response in the United States and United Kingdom—and a tool that continued to be utilized even as market conditions stabilized—was quantitative easing (QE), in other words, central bank asset purchases. QE can not only reduce strains in financial markets, but also provide additional stimulus by reducing medium- and longer-term interest rates.[6] In most economies QE was implemented via purchasing government bonds, but in some cases central banks also purchased mortgage- and asset-backed securities, corporate bonds, municipal bonds, and other types of bonds. It was initially unclear whether QE would have a meaningful impact, but as initial assessments suggested asset purchases provided at least some support, countries doubled down, announcing new rounds of QE and often expanding the scope or introducing new structures, or both. For example, the ECB and Riksbank launched QE programs in the mid-2010s, and the Federal Reserve announced additional QE programs (three in total over 2008–2012), plus an "Operation Twist" that swapped long-term U.S. Treasury bonds for shorter-duration Treasury bonds to flatten the yield curve.

Moreover, as central banks experimented with different types of QE programs, evidence emerged that QE reduced yields for bonds in general (including those that were not directly purchased as part of the program), but caused significantly larger declines in yields for the assets that were eligible for purchase.[7] This applied to different categories of bonds (such as mortgage-backed securities or government bonds) as well as to the specific types of bonds within an asset class (such as whether corporate bonds met specific criteria that made them eligible for the purchase program). In other words, the design of the QE program can determine if certain sectors or companies receive relatively more support.

When the global pandemic began in 2020, central banks quickly revived many of these "unconventional" maneuvers—particularly given the importance of responding quickly as economies were locked down and financial markets froze up. They also substantially expanded the scale, speed, and scope of many programs. These multifaceted and aggressive responses included: rate cuts and forward guidance; asset purchases; liquidity provision and credit support; foreign exchange policies; and regulatory easing. Figure 5.2 shows this array of tactics employed in advanced economies and emerging markets. In one year, March 2020 through March 2021, countries announced: "527 interest rate changes, 59 adjustments in reserve requirements and reserve remuneration rates, 143 lending support actions, 101

		Advanced Economies											Middle East and Africa							
Tool type	**Measures**	US	EA	JP	GB	CA	AU	CH	DK	NO	NZ	SE	AE	DZ	IL	KW	MA	SA	TR	ZA
Interest	Policy rate cut	✓			✓	✓	✓			✓	✓	✓	✓	✓	✓	✓	✓	✓	✓	✓
Lending operations	Liquidity provision	✓	✓	✓	✓	✓	✓		✓	✓	✓	✓		✓	✓	✓	✓	✓	✓	✓
	Targeted lending	✓	✓	✓	✓		✓	✓			✓	✓	✓	✓					✓	✓
Asset purchases[1]	Government bonds	✓	✓	✓	✓	✓	✓				✓	✓			✓				✓	✓
	Commercial paper	✓	✓	✓	✓	✓						✓								
	Corporate bonds	✓	✓	✓	✓	✓						✓			✓					
	Other private		✓	✓		✓						✓								
Foreign exchange	USD swap line		✓	✓	✓	✓	✓	✓	✓	✓	✓	✓								
	Swaps[2]														✓					
	Spot intervention							✓												✓
Reserve policy	Remuneration						✓	✓		✓										✓
	Requirement ratio	✓											✓	✓						
	Compliance																			✓

		Emerging Asia										Latin America						Eastern Europe			
Tool type	**Measures**	CN	HK	ID	IN	KR	MY	PH	SG	TH	VN	AR	BR	CL	CO	MX	PE	CZ	HU	PL	RO
Interest	Policy rate cut	✓	✓	✓	✓	✓	✓	✓		✓	✓	✓	✓	✓	✓	✓	✓	✓	✓	✓	✓
Lending operations	Liquidity provision	✓	✓	✓	✓	✓		✓		✓			✓	✓	✓	✓	✓	✓	✓	✓	✓
	Targeted lending	✓			✓	✓	✓	✓	✓	✓	✓	✓	✓	✓		✓	✓		✓		
Asset purchases[1]	Government bonds		✓	✓	✓			✓		✓				✓	✓			✓	✓		✓
	Commercial paper					✓															
	Corporate bonds				✓					✓									✓		
	Other private													✓	✓				✓		
Foreign exchange	USD swap line					✓			✓				✓			✓					
	Swaps[2]			✓						✓		✓	✓	✓	✓	✓			✓		
	Spot intervention		✓	✓										✓				✓			
Reserve policy	Remuneration	✓		✓																	
	Requirement ratio	✓	✓	✓	✓		✓	✓				✓	✓		✓	✓	✓				✓
	Compliance						✓	✓				✓	✓								✓

[1] Includes operations conducted with assets of different maturity or risk profile (i.e., Operation Twist and swap operations).
[2] Includes nondeliverable forwards.

Figure 5.2
Central bank responses to the 2020 COVID-19 pandemic by tool. *Source*: Figure replicates table 1 from Cantú et al. (2021).

actions related to exchange rate policy (including swap lines), and 54 asset purchase operations" (from Buiter at al. 2023, based on the data in Cantú et al. 2021). Bergant and Forbes (2023b) and English, Forbes, and Ubide (2021) also provide excellent summaries of central bank actions during this period.

For many countries, a key component of this more forceful response was initiating or expanding QE programs, or both.[8] Central bank asset holdings in several major advanced economies jumped in response to the pandemic—including in a number of countries that had not previously used QE (such as Canada and New Zealand). Cantú et al. (2021) report that twenty-one central banks purchased public assets and thirteen purchased private assets (in their sample of forty central banks). The Federal Reserve and Bank of

Japan (BoJ) announced unlimited purchases of government bonds—at even faster rates than in the past. The ECB expanded the size of its main asset purchase program (the APP),[9] and then created a new program to purchase private and public assets (the Pandemic Emergency Purchase Programme, or PEPP) and later another program "to counter unwarranted, disorderly market dynamics that pose a serious threat to the transmission of monetary policy across all [E]uro area countries" (the Transmission Protection Instrument, or TPI).[10] Many emerging markets also introduced APPs (including Hungary, India, Indonesia, Korea, the Philippines, Poland, Romania, South Africa, Thailand, and Turkey), with a mix of goals related to supporting activity, liquidity, or the monetary policy transmission mechanism.

While most economies responded aggressively to the pandemic, different countries employed different combinations of tactics, following Sun Tzu's advice to adapt to the specific foe. Bergant and Forbes (2023b) highlights how each country's combinations of policy responses reflected its individual characteristics, particularly its preexisting policy space for each tool. For example, just over half of the emerging markets and three advanced economies (Iceland, Israel, and Switzerland) reported using currency intervention during the first half of 2020, with countries with lower preexisting reserve levels less likely to intervene.[11] Of the countries choosing to intervene in foreign exchange (FX) markets, about half bought FX and about half sold, while some intervened in small amounts and others with massive interventions (such as Switzerland, which increased reserves by 10.8 percent of GDP).[12] Each country's actions reflected a combination of their initial FX reserve holdings (their "terrain"), as well as maneuvers chosen to respond to the specific situation, including how the crisis was affecting their exchange rate and currency markets.

All in all, central banks relied much more heavily on this set of "unconventional" tools in response to the pandemic than after the GFC.[13] Boone and Rawdanowicz (2021) calculate that the median advanced economy reduced interest rates by just over 4 percentage points in response to the GFC, but reduced rates by only 0.75 percentage points in response to the pandemic. In contrast, asset purchase programs were used much more aggressively. This shift in tactics reflected more than just the constraint of having limited room to lower policy interest rates (and no room in some cases). The severe financial stress in the spring of 2020 required more direct market support than could be provided through reducing interest rates.

Central banks had recently learned about the efficacy of different tools to address different stresses, and the tepid recovery over the last decade had underscored the need to respond forcefully to a shock from "heaven." Also important, after a decade of subtarget inflation, central banks were confident that the Phillips curve was flat and there was minimal risk of inflation picking up sharply.

There was also a subtle but important change in how central banks sequenced using this broader array of tools over the financial battles of the last two decades. In response to the GFC, central banks only announced asset purchase programs after they had lowered policy interest rates to what were believed to be lower bounds; countries that had not lowered interest rates to lower bounds (such as Australia and New Zealand) did not launch asset purchase programs. In response to the pandemic, however, several central banks jumped directly to asset purchases, including several that could have lowered rates further. For example, Sweden had raised interest rates to 0 percent in January 2020 (from a low of –0.50 percent as recently as January 2019), and then responded to the pandemic in March 2020 by launching a new QE program and program to support bank lending to companies—without lowering interest rates. In fact, no central bank cut policy rates to negative levels in response to the pandemic, and for central banks with policy rates that were already negative, none cut them further. A number of central banks in emerging markets also started asset purchase programs despite having policy interest rates well above 0 percent (such as India, Indonesia, Philippines, Poland, South Africa, and Turkey).

Did this change in maneuvers and shift to "unconventional" tools make sense? From a practical standpoint, some central banks had little choice. Their preferred weapon—reducing policy interest rates—only had limited firepower. Even if there had been more ammunition in this weapon, reductions in interest rates may not have provided the liquidity and market support needed, and when markets stabilized, a substantial amount of stimulus was required. Moreover, empirical evidence suggests that QE provides greater stimulus during periods of financial stress.[14] As a result, at the start of the pandemic when liquidity dried up, asset purchases were a logical substitute for reducing policy interest rates (and potentially even the best weapon). As financial markets stabilized, however, the case for relying more on these "unconventional" tools was weaker, particularly in countries with the ability to further reduce rates. Although QE provides some boost to economic activity and inflation even when markets are functioning normally, this can generate a meaningful fiscal cost later on (as discussed in chapter 7), as well as political cost. QE can also constrain a central bank's ability to maneuver if inflation picks up quickly (as discussed in chapter 6). As a result, although this change in tactics prioritizing "unconventional" policies may have made sense during the early stage of the pandemic and for economies with no room to lower interest rates, the case was weaker in 2021 after markets had stabilized and economies bounced back.

Maneuvering During Recoveries and Inflation: Rate Hikes and QT

While central banks have been innovative and aggressive in responding to the recessions and financial crises over the last two decades, they have been more hesitant in responding to periods of recovery and accelerating inflation. Part of this simply reflects the economic backdrop; from 2008 through 2021, most advanced economies struggled with tepid growth and subtarget inflation. They were more concerned about derailing the recovery than overheating or high inflation. It is only since 2021 and 2022 that many central banks began to adjust their multiple weapons during a strong recovery. Since then, they have learned important lessons on how to best combine their two main tools of raising interest rates and unwinding asset holdings through quantitative tightening (QT).

When central banks began using QE more widely in response to the GFC, the asset purchases were intended to be temporary. Central banks planned to start unwinding these purchases through QT once the economic recovery was on track and soon after they started raising policy interest rates. The slow recovery, subpar inflation, and then the Euro area crisis, however, prevented many central banks from being able to maintain increases in interest rates. As shown in figure 5.1, many central banks never even raised rates in the decade after the GFC, and of the advanced economies that initially raised rates after 2008, many then had to reverse course.

Central banks were even slower to start QT throughout the 2010s, partly due to this delay in the perceived prior step of raising policy rates, but also due to uncertainty about its effects. This uncertainty was aggravated by the "taper tantrum" in 2013, when the Federal Reserve suggested it would slow its pace of QE in the future, triggering a sharp negative market reaction including a spike in U.S. Treasury yields and capital outflows and currency depreciations in emerging markets. If the effects of QT were comparable to those of QE (with the sign reversed), unwinding asset holdings could derail the tepid recovery and prevent central banks from raising interest rates much above their lower bounds (which was a priority so they would have room to use this tool to combat future recessions). Central banks were so cautious about starting QT that the United States was the only country to announce QT and make meaningful progress before the pandemic in 2020.[15] This preference for raising policy interest rates instead of starting QT made sense in the 2010s for a number of reasons: (1) adjusting policy interest rates was straightforward to implement and calibrate, as central banks had used this tool for decades in different economic environments and thereby had a better (albeit still far from perfect) understanding of the effects; (2) given the nonexistent experience with QT, it was very hard to calibrate the impact and appropriate size of a program; and (3) with interest rates expected to stay low for an extended period, there appeared to be little cost for central banks to maintain large asset holdings indefinitely (as discussed in more detail in chapter 7).

In the post-pandemic recovery, however, central banks faced a very different battlefield situation. As economic activity bounced back and inflation spiked, it became clear that monetary policy would need to be tightened by a meaningful amount—and much more than over the prior decade. This gave central banks the confidence to launch QT programs, despite substantial uncertainty about the effects. Even if QT led to a significant tightening in financial conditions or had other contractionary effects, it would no longer constrain the ability of central banks to raise interest rates meaningfully above zero given the amount of ground they had to cover. Moreover, if QT began to have meaningful negative effects on market functioning, it could be paused or ended quickly (as occurred in the United States in 2019).

This prompted a number of central banks to begin QT programs in 2022, not only much earlier, but also more aggressively than expected. Figure 5.3 (based on Du, Forbes, and Luzzetti 2024) shows this compressed timetable for the usual maneuvers: first end QE, then "liftoff" (the first rate hike), then start passive QT (allowing the bonds to roll off when they mature), and in some cases then begin active QT (selling bonds before they expire). The left of the figure shows the timeline for the only previous experience with QT; the United States took thirty-six months between ending QE and starting QT, and twenty-two months from lifting off to starting QT. In sharp

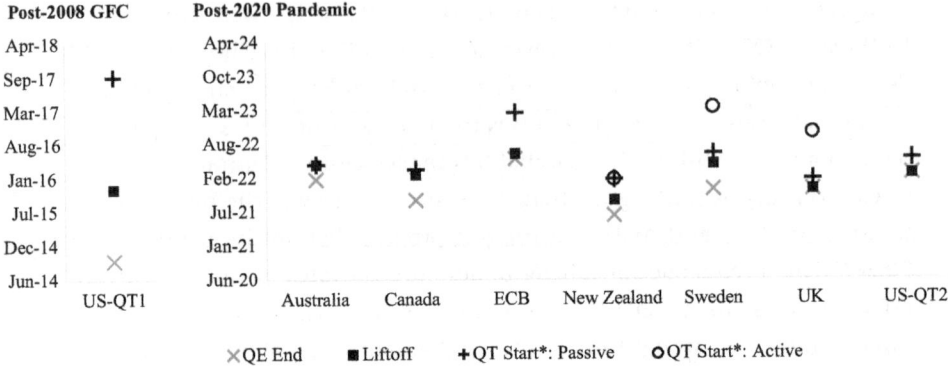

Figure 5.3
Key dates in the monetary policy playbook: QE, liftoff, and QT. *Note*: Figure shows the dates that central banks announced the end to QE, liftoff (the first hike in interest rates), or start of QT (either passive or active). These announcements refer to news on QE and QT programs for government securities and do not capture other changes in central bank balance sheets that are not part of these programs. Dates are based on central bank communications. *Source*: Replicated from figure 2.2 in Du, Forbes, and Luzzetti (2024).

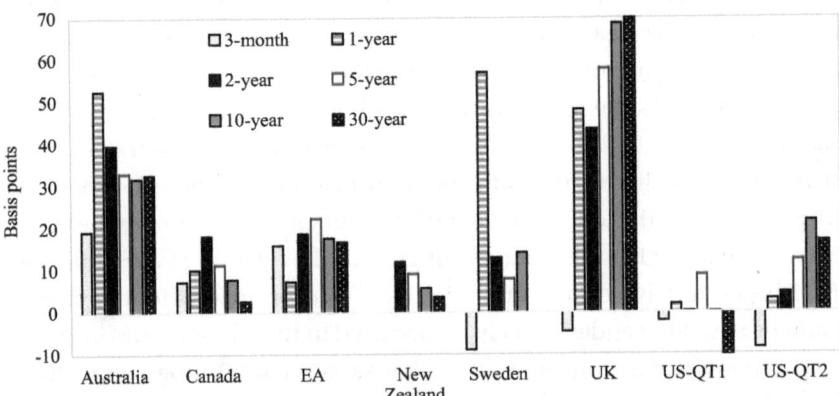

Figure 5.4
Cumulative effects of all QT announcements on government bond yields. *Note*: Calculated as the sum of the estimated effects of each QT announcement by economy through March 2024. These aggregate effects only include QT events that are new or additional QT after 2020, except for the U.S. announcements from 2014 to 2017, which are included as US-QT1. *Source*: Replicated from figure 3.4 in Du, Forbes, and Luzzetti (2024).

contrast, as the recovery took hold after the pandemic, seven central banks quickly announced QT programs, starting just seven months after ending QE (on average) and three months after lifting off. Some central banks were even faster to adjust tactics. For example, the BoE ended QE and simultaneously raised rates for the first time in December 2021, and then started QT at its next meeting. The Reserve Bank of Australia ended QE in February 2022, and then simultaneously raised rates and announced the start of QT at its May 2022 meeting. The faster pace of QT also contributed to meaningful progress shrinking balance sheets. Du, Forbes, and Luzzetti (2024) calculate that the central banks in their sample had already reduced their asset holdings by about one-quarter from their peaks in mid-2022 through the end of 2023, with plans for an additional reduction of about one-quarter by the end of 2025.[16]

This willingness by central banks to move forward with QT sooner and at a faster pace than expected was impressive given the substantial uncertainty about its effects, including how this maneuver would interact with ongoing increases in policy interest rates. Could QT act as a substitute for rate hikes? If the contractionary effects of QT were large, this could imply smaller increases in policy interest rates and the corresponding short-term borrowing and lending rates. This could have important benefits in terms of reducing the risks from rapid (and largely unexpected) increases in borrowing costs for loans linked to these short-term rates (such as credit card debt and bank loans to small businesses). If QT had a larger impact on longer-term interest rates (as found for QE), it would shift some of the adjustment from tighter monetary policy to sectors more exposed to the medium- and longer-end of the yield curve (such as mortgages and borrowing for large companies).[17] If the contractionary effects of QT were small and did not meaningfully substitute for rate hikes (on any portion of the yield curve), central banks could at least mitigate political concerns about large balance sheets and reduce the fiscal costs of holding assets in a higher interest rate environment.

While central banks did not know how QT would interact with rate hikes when they launched these programs in 2022, we now have answers.[18] Du, Forbes, and Luzzetti (2024) assess the cross-country experience with QT and find several key results: (1) QT announcements correspond to a small increase in government bond yields and convenience yields,[19] and in some cases a decline in corporate bond indices; (2) the implementation of QT (when the bonds roll off or are sold) corresponds to a modest rise in overnight funding spreads and a reduction in convenience yields; (3) the impact of QT on most other financial market measures is also consistent with a tightening in financial conditions, but the effect is usually small and statistically insignificant; and (4) active QT primarily affects yields at longer horizons (thereby steepening the yield curve) and corporate bonds, while passive QT primarily effects yields at shorter horizons (thereby flattening the curve) and the convenience yield.

All in all, this series of results suggests that the effects of QT tend to be small and are much more muted than for QE, although much of this more subdued impact reflects the more tranquil market conditions when QT programs were launched (as compared to QE, which generates the largest effects during periods of market stress). More specifically, Du, Forbes, and Luzzetti (2024) find that, on average, an announcement of new or additional QT corresponds to a small but significant increase in government bond yields of about 4 to 8 basis points at horizons of one year and longer (and this is probably an underestimate as some of the impact was likely priced in ahead of time in countries where QT was expected). Figure 5.4 shows the corresponding cumulative effects of all QT announcements through the end of 2023, with the aggregate impact ranging from almost nothing in the United States to an increase in government bond yields of 44–69 basis points in the United Kingdom.[20] On average, these cumulated effects of all QT announcements are an increase of 21 basis points in ten-year government bond yields (through 2023).

How do these effects of QT compare with those of the "conventional" strategy of raising policy interest rate rates over this period? To put these two maneuvers in perspective, figure 5.5 shows the path of policy interest rates in the same group of countries over the same period (discussed in more detail in chapter 6) and then redraws figure 5.4 to use the same scale for the two graphs (i.e., with 100 basis points equal to 1 percent.). This comparison clearly shows that even though QT tightened financial conditions, its modest effects were dominated by the impact of raising interest rates.

To conclude, this recent experience with QT has shown that adjusting policy interest rates is more effective at tightening financial conditions than QT, especially if a large adjustment is required. Achieving a specific amount of tightening in financial conditions is also easier to calibrate by adjusting policy rates. Relying on QT is more challenging, as it is not only harder to calibrate (especially given the wide range of effects across countries), but

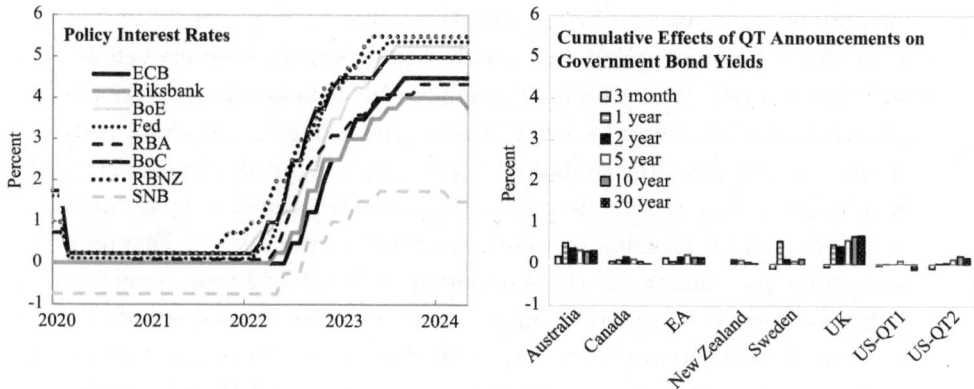

Figure 5.5
Impact of two tightening tools: policy rates and QT (2020–2024). *Note*: Left panel is an excerpt of figure 5.1 for the subperiod from January 2020 through March 2024. Right panel replicates figure 5.4, except resets the axis to mirror that of the panel on the left, i.e., based on percentage points instead of basis points. See notes to figures 5.1 and 5.4 for definitions. *Sources*: Data for policy rates from BIS, Haver, and OECD. Data for effects of QT from figure 3.4 in Du, Forbes, and Luzzetti (2024).

also, if a large tightening in financial conditions is required, the requisite reductions in central bank asset holdings would be so large that there could be risks to financial stability if QT was the only tool employed. In the recent battle against inflation, increases in policy interest rates were clearly a more effective weapon than reducing central bank balance sheets.

Maneuvering in Different States of the World: Lessons for the Future

This experience with conventional and unconventional tools over the last two decades has provided central banks with useful new information on different tactics for easing and tightening monetary policy, and especially how to combine the weapons of adjusting policy interest rates and balance sheets. This experience provides important insights on how to prioritize the use of these different maneuvers in the future.

A first lesson is that the "conventional" tool of adjusting policy interest rates—during recessions as well as recoveries—should usually be the first maneuver if rates are not already at their lower bounds. Reducing rates is the most effective tool during recessions, and raising rates is most effective during recoveries, to achieve monetary policy goals such as price stability and supporting economic activity. QE and QT can also support these goals, but their effects are more muted, particularly during periods when markets are functioning normally and liquidity is ample. The main exception to relying primarily on adjustments to policy interest rates is during a financial crisis when severe market stress or illiquidity threatens the broader financial system. In this case, asset purchases as part of short-term emergency facilities to support market functioning may be required (as discussed in chapter 2 and Cantú et al. 2021), but these should be differentiated from monetary policy tools aimed at supporting price stability and economic activity. Macroprudential tools (discussed in chapter 4) can also be adjusted to support changes in interest rates (such as cutting regulatory capital and liquidity buffers during a downturn, and tightening them during a recovery), but the effects on lending and activity are modest, and much larger adjustments than currently have political support would be required to replace the tool of adjusting policy interest rates.[21]

A second lesson, however, is that even if QE is a "second-class" tool that should generally only be used in periods of severe financial stress or if reducing policy rates is not viable, QT should <u>not</u> be relegated to second-class status and only used if the ability to adjust rates is exhausted. This is not just because there is technically no "upper bound" after which interest rates could no longer be raised (comparable to the lower bound for rates after which QE may be the best option). Instead, since the effects of QT appear to be so small (at least in periods of ample liquidity), QT can usually occur in the background and in conjunction with a range of other tactics. QT has had such a minimal impact to date that it can be used not only when central banks are raising interest rates, but also when they shift to reducing rates. In fact, most of the seven advanced economies with ongoing QT programs discussed previously reduced their policy interest rates during 2024 while continuing their QT programs—with no apparent challenges in communication or disruptions to either policy.

There is one critically important caveat, however, to this lesson that QT can run quietly in the background: as liquidity balances decline, QT could suddenly have a more meaningful impact and generate a sharp tightening in financial conditions. Although this has not occurred in any economy pursuing QT as of mid-2024, the U.S. experience with QT in 2019 was a warning that the impact of QT can be nonlinear and accelerate as reserve balances decline.[22] If QT does suddenly start to have a larger impact on financial conditions—even if reflecting an interaction with "heavenly" shocks and not just the direct impact of QT—any such balance sheet reductions should be slowed, paused, or stopped.

Barring any financial stability concerns, this ability to continue QT "in the background" while adjusting rates in either direction is an important asymmetry in how conventional and unconventional tools can be combined during recessions and recoveries. As discussed in more detail in chapter 6, if a country has a QE program in place, it can be difficult to pivot and raise interest rates quickly, limiting the flexibility of central banks to adjust when the macroeconomic environment changes. In contrast, having a QT program in place does not constrain a central bank's ability to quickly change tactics and shift to cutting interest rates. Central banks have been effective at messaging that QT is not the primary tool for adjusting monetary policy—so it can continue in the background while interest rates are adjusted as needed in either direction to provide the appropriate degree of monetary stimulus. As a result, central banks should not be as cautious about starting QT and shrinking balance sheets in the future.

A final lesson is the importance of thinking carefully about exactly which assets are included in balance sheet programs and how the program is structured, particularly given the evidence that the assets included in QE programs benefit from additional stimulus. Central banks should generally focus purchases on large, liquid government bond markets that are more directly linked to broader financial conditions. They should not be involved in allocation decisions across specific industries or companies. When central banks diverge from this strategy, there should be a clear justification of why a specific sector or group of companies merits additional support. For example, it made sense for the Federal Reserve to buy mortgage-backed securities (MBS) during the GFC, as housing was at the core of the systemic financial vulnerabilities and supporting the housing market was central to stabilizing financial markets and supporting a broader economic recovery. However, there was less of a case to include MBS as part of QE during 2021 (after the initial period of financial turmoil around the start of the pandemic) as the housing market boomed and appeared to be more at risk of overheating (and contributing to future vulnerabilities), rather than of collapsing.

Similarly, when designing QT programs, central banks should consider how to prioritize unwinding different types of assets. Holdings of nongovernment assets should be unwound first (assuming this does not generate risks to market functioning), in order to avoid appearing to give preference to certain companies, sectors, or municipalities. This is particularly important for any ownership of corporate bonds or equities, as the central bank would not want to be linked to an individual entity that experienced negative headlines (for whatever reason). Central banks should also evaluate whether to prioritize reducing balance sheets through passive QT (which has a larger impact on short-term yields) or active QT (which has a larger impact on long-term yields). Active QT can help reduce balance sheets more quickly, but generates larger immediate fiscal costs for central banks that do not mark-to-market the value of their asset holdings (discussed in more detail in chapter 7).

To conclude, central banks have made impressive progress in developing multifaceted new strategies over the last two decades. They have also learned a substantial amount about how to use their new weapons, including how to sequence and combine their application. While the traditional strategy of adjusting interest rates still appears to be the most effective weapon for most circumstances, there are situations when having additional weapons in the arsenal is not only useful, but critical to mitigate losses (such as during a financial crisis).

6 Modifying and Varying Tactics: Maintaining Flexibility

While Sun Tzu highlights the importance of planning ahead (chapter 2), he does not mean establishing a fixed course. Instead, he continually highlights the importance of adjusting strategies for each situation and maintaining flexibility in order to be able to quickly adjust to different contingencies. Given the importance of shocks from "heaven" that are outside anyone's control (chapter 3), the situation encountered may be very different from what was expected and planned for. Moreover, even if the shocks were expected and occurred before, they could be transmitted in different ways. A general or central bank must be able to adjust and pivot quickly. The maneuvers and strategy that proved successful in one situation may not be optimal in the next skirmish.

> He who can modify his tactics in relation to his opponent and thereby succeed in winning, may be called a heaven-born captain. (Sun Tzu, *The Art of War*, Chapter 6, Principle 33)

> Do not repeat the tactics which have gained you one victory, but let your methods be regulated by the infinite variety of circumstances. (Sun Tzu, *The Art of War*, Chapter 6, Principle 28)

> So, the student of war who is unversed in the art of war of varying his plans, even though he be acquainted with the Five Advantages, will fail to make the best use of his men. (Sun Tzu, *The Art of War*, Chapter 8, Principle 6)

Over the last two decades, central banks have been adept at modifying their tactics and maintaining flexibility after sharp negative shocks to economic activity and periods of extreme stress in financial markets. They have been less nimble, however, in adjusting to rebounds in activity and spikes in inflation. This chapter discusses when central banks showed the agility recommended by Sun Tzu, followed by when they were less nimble, and then ends with several recommendations for how central banks could improve their flexibility in the future, particularly in response to positive economic surprises.

Recent Examples of Flexibility and Varying Tactics

Central banks have been remarkably resourceful at responding to the major wars of the last two decades: the 2008 GFC and 2020 COVID-19 pandemic (Bernanke 2020). As discussed in detail in chapter 5, central banks quickly jumped into action in each case when financial markets froze up and economic activity was collapsing. Most combined the traditional weapon of reducing interest rates (at least for economies that had space) with a varied array of "unconventional" weapons and tactics. After developing many of these tactics in response to the 2008 crisis, they not only revived them in 2020, but expanded them in terms of the size, speed, and scope of assets purchased and markets supported.

These multifaceted central bank responses to the GFC and the pandemic would likely be praised by Sun Tzu. Central banks not only "modified their tactics," but introduced a series of innovative new programs and strategies. They constantly adapted their strategies to the "infinite variety of circumstances," particularly in response to unprecedented strains resulting from the nature of the pandemic (as compared to most historical crises, which correspond to overheating and excess leverage followed by a financial crisis). Central banks were also nimble in adapting their tools to accomplish multidimensional and changing goals; for example, asset purchases were initially launched to address widespread dysfunction in key financial markets, and later used to support aggregate demand and achieve price stability.

Moreover, although a number of central banks adopted a "whatever it takes" approach, they also followed Sun Tzu's principle of not applying tactics from previous battles if they did not make sense for "the foe whom he is facing." For example, most central banks avoided adjusting capital controls or adopting negative interest rates (as discussed in chapter 5). Future generations can debate whether the totality of the responses qualifies for Tzu's "heaven-born captain," but central banks displayed noteworthy adaptability and flexibility in modifying their tactics in response to the major crises of the last two decades.

Recent Examples of Inflexibility and a Delayed Modification in Tactics

In contrast to this impressive flexibility and modification in tactics in response to the severe negative shocks of the GFC and the pandemic, central banks were less nimble in responding to the rapid recovery and subsequent spike in inflation after 2020. Demand rebounded faster than expected after the COVID-19 lockdowns ended, supported by the rapid rollout and effectiveness of the vaccines and the highly expansionary mix of monetary policy (discussed earlier) and fiscal policy. This rapid rebound interacted with a series of unprecedented supply-side shocks from the shutdown and then reopening of the global economy and broad-based increases in commodity prices after the invasion of Ukraine (English, Forbes, and Ubide 2024). This combination of factors caused inflation to spike to levels not seen since the mid-1980s (figure 3.2)—reaching an average of about 8 percent in advanced economies in 2022. This surge in inflation was widespread, with 96 percent of the advanced economies reporting inflation above 2.5 percent in 2022 and 92 percent in 2023 (figure 3.4). Potentially more disconcerting, the inflation overshoot was substantial not just for CPI inflation (which could largely reflect transitory shocks to energy and food prices), but also for core inflation. Figure 6.1 shows

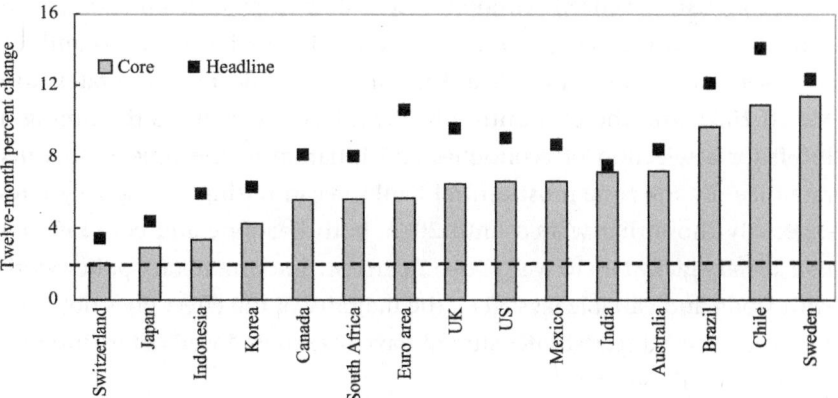

Figure 6.1

Peak inflation: 2020–2023. *Note*: Economies are ordered by their peak core inflation rates. Core inflation for most economies refers to all items excluding food and energy. For Indonesia, core is all items excluding food. For Australia, data is the monthly CPI indicator rather than the quarterly CPI, and core excludes volatile items and holiday travel. *Source*: Replicated from figure 6 in chapter 1 in English, Forbes, and Ubide (2024). Original data from World Bank, Global Inflation Database, OECDStat, and National Sources.

the peak in both CPI and core inflation for fifteen economies between 2020 and 2023; headline inflation peaked at more than 8 percent in most of the advanced economies, and core inflation was more than triple the inflation target in major economies such as the United States, the United Kingdom, Sweden, and Australia.

Central banks were slow to realize that this pick up in inflation was more than just a short-lived supply shock.[1] Forecasts (by everyone—and not just central banks) continually missed the acceleration in inflation, even after the Russia invasion of Ukraine caused energy and other commodity prices to spike. As inflation rose to higher levels for much longer than expected, there was a risk that inflation expectations would become unanchored, and the price increases (even if initially temporary) would have more prolonged effects on wage and price setting.

Emerging markets, particularly those with a more recent history of high inflation or less well-anchored inflation expectations, or both, were the first to respond and modify their tactics. Many began to tighten monetary policy early in 2021, including Brazil in March, quickly followed by Mexico and Chile. By the end of 2021, most emerging markets had not only "lifted off," but tightened policy meaningfully. For example, Brazil had raised its policy interest rate by 725 basis points by the end of 2021.

In contrast, advanced economies were slow to pivot from easing monetary policy. At the end of 2021, most were still purchasing assets and had not even raised rates once.[2] The Federal Reserve did not raise rates until March 2022, and the ECB until July 2022. Figure 6.2 shows the timing of liftoff for a selection of economies and inflation at the time of this first rate hike. By the time most central banks began raising their policy rates, especially those that waited until 2022, both headline and core inflation had already picked up to well above 2 percent. Since monetary policy works with "long and variable lags" (i.e., the majority of the effect does not occur for over a year), interest rates should have been raised well before inflation had reached these levels.

A comparison of macroeconomic variables other than inflation also provides evidence that central banks were slow to pivot from easing to tightening monetary policy after the pandemic. For example, figure 6.3 (replicated from Forbes, Ha, and Kose 2024b) compares the evolution of employment, unemployment, GDP, and industrial production (IP) during

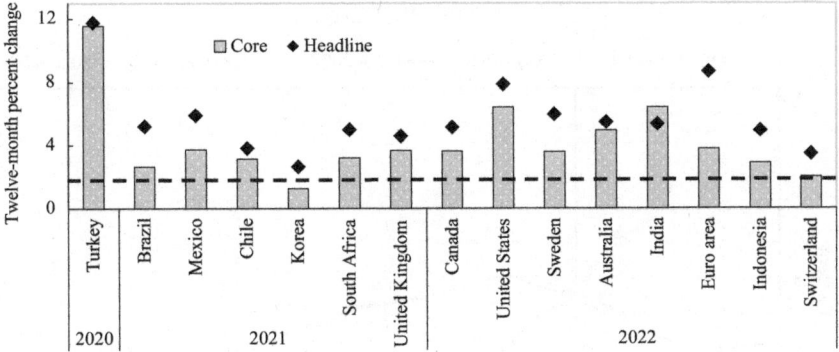

Figure 6.2

Inflation at liftoff. *Note*: Economies are ordered by the date of liftoff (i.e., the first rate hike). Core inflation for most economies refers to all items excluding food and energy. See notes for figure 6.1 for details on definitions. *Source*: Replicated from figure 6 in chapter 1 in English, Forbes, and Ubide (2024). Original data from World Bank, Global Inflation Database, OECDStat, and National Sources.

tightening cycles in advanced economies over historical windows from January 1970 through March 2024. In each case, t = 0 is the start of each "tightening cycle" (i.e., the first increase in the policy interest rate after an easing period).[3] The post-pandemic tightening cycle (in the thick black line) clearly stands out. During earlier tightening phases, monetary policy was first tightened when each measure of activity was substantially weaker than in 2021–2022. Central banks delayed tightening after the pandemic until each measure of activity was unusually strong.

After this slow start and post-pandemic inflation overshoot, central banks then had to tighten monetary policy faster than historical norms. The post-pandemic tightening was more aggressive than historical tightening cycles since 1999 by most measures—such as the number of rate increases, total magnitude of rate hikes, average speed of rate hikes, and initial velocity of rate hikes (Forbes, Ha, and Kose 2024b). This subsequently caused a faster deterioration in the different measures of activity and the labor market than has historically occurred. This pattern is also evident in figure 6.3; in each historical tightening cycle, the first rate hike weakens activity after a lag of roughly a year (and longer for labor markets), but this deterioration was sharper after the unusually aggressive post-pandemic tightening.

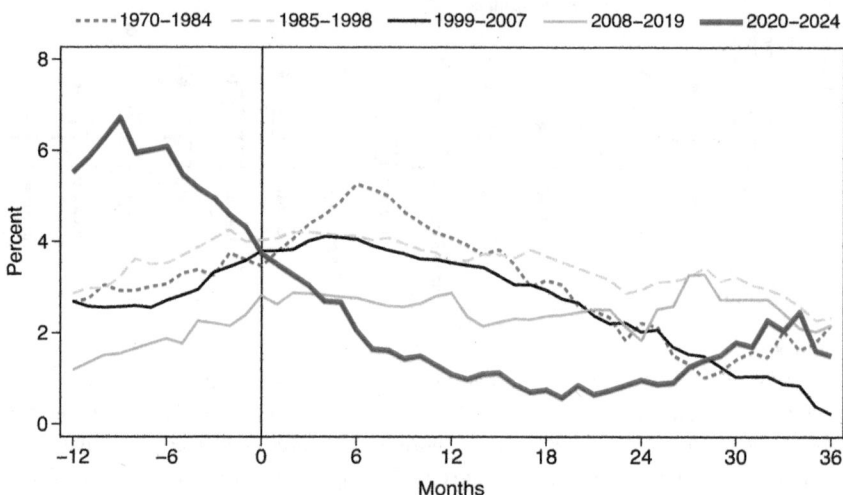

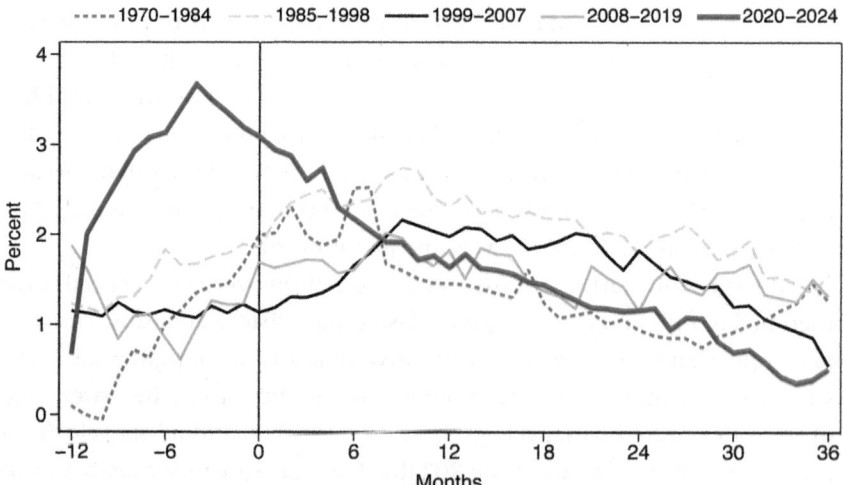

Figure 6.3
Economic activity and the labor market during historical tightening cycles. *Note*:
Graphs show the median of each variable during tightening cycles that occurred
during the historical windows listed at the bottom. The *t* is set to zero at the first rate
hike at the start of the tightening phase. All variables are calculated as the percent
change relative to twelve months earlier, except for the unemployment rate, which

Industrial Production Growth

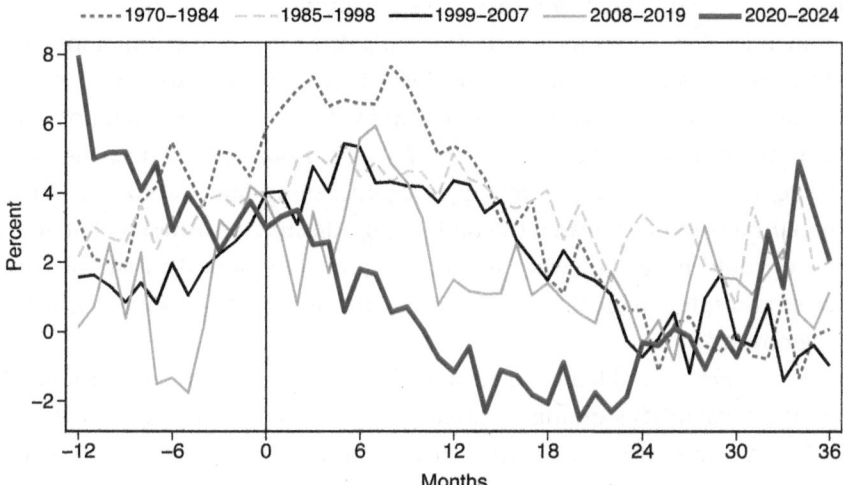

Unemployment Rate (12m change)

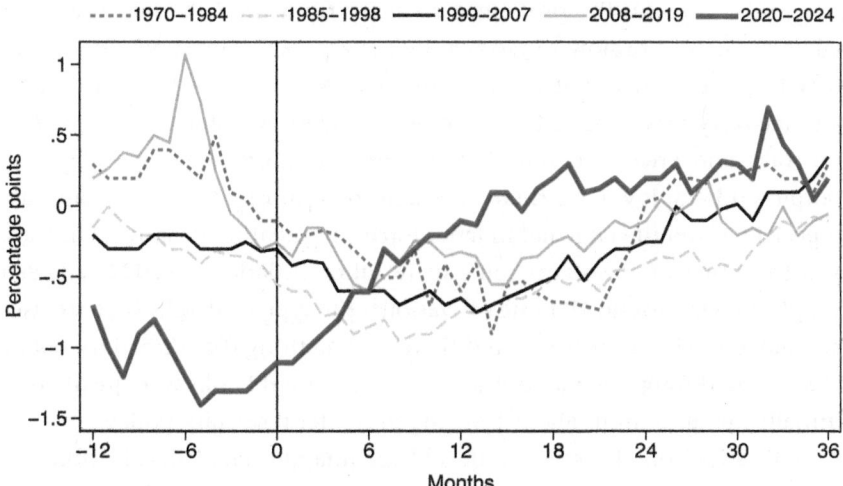

is the change. Phases are defined based on individual Euro area countries through 1998, and then for the ECB starting in 1999, with the corresponding macroeconomic variables then based on the Euro area (and not individual countries). See Forbes, Ha, and Kose (2024a) for additional details on data sources and calculations. *Source*: Excerpt from chart 8 in Forbes, Ha, and Kose (2024a).

These patterns suggest that if central banks had been more flexible and pivoted more quickly from easing to tightening monetary policy after the pandemic, they could have not only mitigated some of the inflation overshoot, but also the subsequent slowdown in activity and labor markets. To be fair, most of the inflation overshoot and swings in activity could not have been avoided given the confluence of shocks from heaven (i.e., the pandemic, Ukraine invasion, and supply chain issues), but the slow response by central banks aggravated the underlying adjustments. A faster change in tactics could have somewhat moderated both the painful inflation overshoot and subsequent slowdown, potentially avoiding a recession in some economies.[4]

Why were central banks in advanced economies so slow to start removing the substantial stimulus in place when the recovery gained steam and inflation picked up? Several factors played a role (and are discussed in much more detail in English, Forbes, and Ubide 2024). First, confidence in the stability of inflation expectations, partly resulting from inflation being below target in most advanced economies for over a decade, was expected to provide an anchor to mitigate any second-round effects from the initial inflation spike. Second, the prolonged recovery from the GFC suggested that labor markets were slow to recover after sharp recessions, and when combined with evidence that the Phillips curve was flat over the last decade, any recovery was expected to have only modest and slow-moving effects on wage and price inflation.[5] Third, after the unprecedented collapse in output and employment, there appeared to be substantial excess capacity, especially given the large fall in labor force participation in some countries. Fourth, much of the sharp spike in headline inflation in 2022 reflected supply shocks around Ukraine's invasion—the type of shocks that are usually judged to be "transitory" and thereby something that monetary policy could look through. For all of these reasons, central banks were justified in initially being cautious about pivoting to tighter monetary policy.

A final reason, however, reflected an unappreciated disadvantage of some of the "unconventional" tools that central banks used over the last two decades: reduced flexibility.[6] The policies and guidance in place from the pandemic response made it more difficult for central banks to quickly adjust tactics and reduce stimulus.[7] Since the post-pandemic recovery was expected to be protracted, the COVID-19 related stimulus included commitments over a longer period than were used in response to the GFC. For example, there was greater use of forward guidance that rates would be low for an extended period, including yield curve control in Australia.[8] Some economies had already committed to a fixed size for larger QE programs; ending these programs early could undermine the credibility of future QE announcements and reduce the potency of this tool. Other major economies had ongoing asset purchase programs with no end date (including the United States) and were worried that suddenly winding down these programs would generate a sharp, negative market reaction. The Federal Reserve was particularly worried that a quick change in strategy could cause another "taper tantrum" with global spillovers.

Potentially even more problematic, these constraints on central banks' ability to end QE programs delayed the start of rate hikes, the key weapon for constraining inflation—a delay that became more of an issue as inflation spiked in early 2021. Although there is no rule against raising interest rates while QE is ongoing, it is difficult to communicate why a central bank is simultaneously easing policy with one tool (QE) while tightening with another (raising rates). Raising rates simultaneously with QE could also undermine the effectiveness of QE in the future, as part of its impact appears to be the signal it provides that policy rates will remain low for an extended period.[9]

Once central banks realized that that they were behind the curve and that inflation would be substantially higher and for longer than expected, however, many quickly pivoted from easing monetary policy to an unusually aggressive tightening cycle. In fact, this was the fastest shift from actively easing monetary policy to raising rates, on average, in any historical cycle (Forbes, Ha, and Kose 2024b). Policy was "on hold" for an average of only three months between when countries were actively providing stimulus (by lowering rates or doing QE) to when they started raising rates, much faster than the average transition of fifteen months since the GFC. This pivot to raising rates was then followed by an unusually aggressive series of rate hikes, and a much faster start to quantitative tightening (QT) than widely expected (discussed earlier in this chapter and in chapter 5).

To date, this delayed shift to an unusually aggressive tightening cycle seems to have largely worked in terms of bringing inflation back down toward targets—at least as of mid-2024. Most macroeconomic variables have also returned to around levels typical of this stage in a tightening cycle, and the sharp recessions many feared have largely been averted. The cost, however, was a longer period of high inflation and corresponding permanent and painful increase in the price level. This has fed political frustration—including dissatisfaction with the performance of central banks. Moreover, such an aggressive and unexpected tightening in monetary policy has created challenges for many households and businesses that made decisions based on guidance that rates would remain low for an extended period. The aggressive tightening also generated strains for some financial institutions (such as the run on Silicon Valley Bank and other U.S. regional banks discussed in chapter 2), requiring the Federal Reserve to step in with yet another new liquidity program. This mini crisis was a poignant reminder that the strategy of being slow to adjust tactics (i.e., raise interest rates) when inflation picked up, and then attempt to compensate for the delay with unusually aggressive rate hikes, can generate a new set of risks (i.e., that "something breaks"). Although this battle strategy may have been largely successful in the post-pandemic war against inflation, it is a risky strategy for the future.

To summarize, central banks have been flexible and quick to adjust tactics in response to the crises and sharp recessions over the last two decades, but slower to pivot in response to the post-pandemic rebound and acceleration in inflation. While this reflected a number of factors, one was constraints from the weapons used in the pandemic response. Some of the "unconventional" tools, which were important in stabilizing economies and financial systems, also slowed central banks' ability to quickly maneuver as the battlefield conditions changed. When multiple weapons are employed, it is important to consider not only how to use each in isolation, but also how they could complicate the use of other tools and strategies. Flexibility is paramount in a world with powerful external shocks from heaven.

Maintaining Flexibility: Suggestions for the Future

While central banks have been remarkably nimble in responding to crises and recessions, are there ways in which they can improve their flexibility and ability to modify tactics during recoveries or more normal times, or both? Even if there are circumstances when committing to maintain a certain policy for an extended period can improve its efficacy, how should any benefits be weighed against the costs of breaking this commitment or not adjusting monetary policy appropriately to achieve a mandate? The discussion in chapter 5 detailing why central banks were slow to pivot away from easing monetary policy when inflation spiked suggests several concrete strategies for improving flexibility in the future—potentially at a minimal cost.

First, when central banks announce new policies—such as asset purchase programs—they should structure the programs so that they can easily be adjusted, amended, and ended if the macroeconomic environment suddenly changes. They should be able to exit the battle if engagement is no longer beneficial. Building in this flexibility is particularly important in periods of substantial macroeconomic uncertainty and given the large and growing role of heavenly shocks (chapter 3). This makes forecasting inflation—a key input for monetary policy decisions—extremely challenging. As a result, any forward guidance or new programs should not be time-dependent (i.e., for a fixed amount of time or quantity) and instead be state-dependent (i.e., based on the state of the economy). By linking the magnitude and duration of the program to the evolution of variables central to monetary policy, it should be easier to change tactics and adjust the program when the economic environment changes.

An example of state-dependent guidance that has worked well is the Bank of England's (BoE's) approach for when to start quantitative tightening (QT). Most central banks provided little (or no) information on when or how they would start to unwind their large asset purchases made under previous QE programs. In contrast, the BoE provided guidance well before any change in policy was expected; it announced it would start passive QT (allowing expiring assets to roll off the balance sheet) when it raised its policy interest rate to 50 basis points, and then consider active sales of government bonds when it raised its policy rate to 100 basis points.[10] By providing this guidance far in advance, investors began to adjust their expectations for QT as the macroeconomic data began to improve, allowing the BoE to avoid an extended period of trying to prepare markets for a change in balance sheet policy. This also allowed the BoE to be the first to start QT after the pandemic (in February 2022)—just one meeting after its first rate hike—and without any disruption in financial markets.

A second and closely related lesson is that if a program is not state-dependent, it should only be planned for a short horizon or limited magnitude—albeit leaving the option open to extend and expand the program if merited by the evolution of the economy. This is particularly important for QE programs, but less so for QT programs (which do not limit a central bank's flexibility to adjust interest rates in either direction, as discussed earlier and in chapter 5). A concrete example is the BoE's approach to QE; in each case it announced a fixed size of asset purchases, and if the program was completed and more stimulus was merited, it announced an additional fixed allotment. Although these fixed program sizes may still last longer than optimal (with the benefit of hindsight), having a default end date makes it easier to end stimulus when no longer needed without creating market turmoil by surprising investors. This strategy should reduce the likelihood of a taper tantrum[11] and avoid the need for awkward messaging to prepare for winding down QE, such as the Federal Reserve's discussion about whether it was "talking about talking about tapering" before "talking about tapering" and then tapering.[12]

A third lesson is to consider the ease of unwinding different types of assets when a central bank is deciding what assets to purchase as part of a QE program. For most countries, the primary method for reducing central bank holdings is passive QT, in other words, allowing holdings to roll off the balance sheet when they mature. The rate of passive run-off varies meaningfully across economies, however, based on the structure and maturity of the holdings. For example, some countries primarily purchased short-duration assets in their QE programs (such as Canada), so the balance sheet subsequently shrinks quickly through passive run-off after QE has ceased. In contrast, central banks with longer-duration assets may need to actively sell assets to meaningfully shrink their balance sheets. Active sales are generally viewed as less desirable as they create more risks of market disruption and have a larger impact on longer-term yields, as well as generating a larger fiscal cost under certain accounting structures.[13]

Several examples highlight how decisions on what assets to include in a QE program a priori can affect the ease of unwinding these purchases ex post. The average maturity of assets purchased during the pandemic by the Bank of Canada (BoC) was 5.9 years, and by the BoE was 13.0 years. The BoC has been able to reduce its balance sheet quickly through only passive run-off and is expected to end QT by the end of 2025.[14] In contrast, the reduction in the BoE's longer-duration balance sheet has been twice as slow, despite starting QT earlier and including a fairly aggressive program of active bond sales (sales which have generated meaningful fiscal losses for the government and are creating political challenges, as discussed in chapter 7).

The recent experience of the U.S. Federal Reserve also shows that the structure of the assets can matter as well as the duration. The Federal Reserve purchased mortgage-backed securities (MBS) as well as government bonds in its QE programs, and has set caps for the maximum amount of each that can run off each month during QT. While enough government bonds mature regularly that their cap is met each month, the MBS have been so slow to run off that they rarely even meet the cap. This slower run-off of MBS reflects the impact of elevated interest rates, which has reduced the incentive for households to move or refinance their mortgages, or both. Future QE programs should learn from these experiences and prioritize buying shorter-term securities (unless there is a clear reason to reduce yields at the longer end of the curve) and purchasing U.S. Treasury securities instead of housing-related debt (barring a clear reason why the housing market needs support).

A final lesson for central banks to improve their flexibility and be able to quickly modify tactics in the future is to keep each meeting "live" and not feel pressure to preannounce monetary policy decisions in advance. As central banks have relied more heavily on forward guidance, many investors became accustomed to central banks signaling changes in monetary policy before the actual decision was voted on and announced. Central banks also feel pressure not to surprise investors and risk a sharp market reaction, especially as they have recently put more emphasis on clear and transparent communication. If central banks signal what they plan to do in advance of each meeting, however, it can be difficult to adjust policy quickly if the macroeconomic environment changes. In a world of large, external shocks from heaven (chapter 3), this can restrict the central banks' ability to maneuver and adjust tactics, especially because there can be meaningful news breaking between when a central bank goes into its quiet period (with no public comments) and when a monetary decision is announced. If central banks provided less guidance, particularly if paired with greater use of scenario analysis highlighting different potential outcomes (as discussed in chapters 3 and 4), this should also encourage investors, households, and companies to better plan for different contingencies. This type of planning should build resilience for a range of outcomes, reinforcing the ability of central banks to quickly adjust tactics in the future.

To conclude, adjusting tactics may be as challenging for central banks in some scenarios as for generals adjusting their battle plans. Yet, in both cases, a last-minute pivot may be the optimal strategy. A careful design of battle plans in advance, however, can help provide this flexibility and facilitate the ability to quickly modify tactics.

7   The Costs of Fighting Battles: Trade-Offs

A key theme throughout Sun Tsu's *The Art of War* is the need to consider the potential costs—as well as the benefits—of various policies. This encompasses not only the direct fiscal costs of any strategy, but also the broader costs for society—including the challenges from "high prices" (i.e., inflation). These trade-offs involve carefully managing resources (of yourself and the opposing side), as well as balancing risker strategies that could shorten the conflict versus lengthier operations that reduce the risk of military losses but could deplete reserves and undermine political support.

> If the campaign is protracted, the resources of the State will not be equal the strain. (Sun Tzu, *The Art of War*, Chapter 2, Principle 3)

> The proximity of an army causes prices to go up; and high prices cause the people's substance to be drained away. (Sun Tzu, *The Art of War*, Chapter 2, Principle 11)

> When their substance is drained away, the peasantry will be afflicted by heavy exactions. (Sun Tzu, *The Art of War*, Chapter 2, Principle 12)

Central banks have recently been reminded of the importance of evaluating these types of costs and trade-offs—particularly related to longer operations and costs that arise after the battle. When central banks launched a series of innovative and "unconventional" policies in response to the GFC (chapter 4), they expected to unwind most of these measures soon after the immediate crisis abated. Not only were most central banks unable to make progress in the subsequent decade, but then they also restarted many of these programs—in even larger scope and scale—in response to the pandemic. Given the extent of the health, economic, and financial crises in 2020, there was a "do whatever it takes" approach and minimal attention to potential costs that could arise in the future. These costs were also easy to downplay as asset purchases over the previous decade had largely been profitable. As interest rates increased, however, these profits turned to losses in many economies and raised awareness of the potential risks from these new tools. This chapter discusses new evidence on these costs and trade-offs, focusing on the lessons learned from the widespread use of asset purchase programs, and then provides several suggestions to ensure these lessons are incorporated in future monetary policy decisions.

The Costs of Unconventional Tactics

There is an extensive literature on the trade-offs when central banks use their "conventional" tool of adjusting interest rates.[1] This evaluation has been possible given the widespread use of this tactic across economies and over time, including in many different environments. There has been less attention, however, to the trade-offs from the new array of "unconventional" tools (discussed in chapter 5). Some of this is understandable. Many of the tools have only been used recently (such as QT)—so only preliminary assessments of the immediate impact are possible and there is minimal information on the longer-term costs in different situations (such as risks from QT when reserve levels are no longer considered "ample," as discussed in Du, Forbes, and Luzzetti 2024). Other tools that were used during the GFC and the pandemic are difficult to assess as so many policies were adopted simultaneously during a period of heightened market volatility, making it impossible to isolate the costs and benefits of any individual action. Many emergency programs were designed and adopted differently across economies and periods, so that it is challenging to draw conclusions using cross-country analysis.

Despite these challenges, we have learned a substantial amount about the potential costs from one of the most prominent new tools used over the last two decades—quantitative easing (QE). As discussed in chapter 5, central banks were slow to unwind the assets they purchased as part of their response to the GFC, European sovereign debt crisis, and subsequent period of subtarget inflation. In fact, the United States was the only economy to make meaningful progress reducing its balance sheet through QT (and even the United States had to stop QT earlier than initially planned). This lack of urgency in unwinding asset purchases was supported by the belief that there was minimal cost to central banks of maintaining large balance sheets—and in some cases a fiscal benefit. Granted, many of these costs are hard to measure, such as any impact on market functioning.[2] Nonetheless, recent economic developments have highlighted how two costs (the "interest rate carry" and changes in bond valuations) can be large and should be considered before a central bank embarks on QE in the future.

The interest rate carry is the difference between the interest rate the central bank earns on its bond holdings (largely from past QE programs) less the interest it pays on bank reserves or overnight repos, or both. In the low interest rate environment that prevailed in the 2010s, this corresponded to meaningful profits for most central banks, as the interest rate on their holdings was higher than what they paid on reserves. When interest rates were increased aggressively after the pandemic (chapters 5 and 6), however, these large profits quickly turned into losses. While central banks had been forthright in warning that this stream of profits from the interest rate carry might not last, they did not foresee how quickly these revenues would reverse or the magnitude of the losses (largely because they did not predict the sharp increases in interest rates).

The other important consideration is capital gains or losses on the value of central bank bond holdings. Central banks pursuing active QT (i.e., selling bonds before they expire), generally experience losses from selling bonds that were purchased as part of QE programs (as they were purchased when rates were near zero, and prices have since fallen as interest rates increased).[3] For central banks that are not actively selling bonds as part of QT, some are still forced to mark-to-market the value of their bonds and thereby record these capital losses on their portfolios (such as the Riksbank and Bank of Canada). For central banks that are only required to account for capital losses when the bonds are sold or mature (such as the UK), this could provide an incentive to delay any reduction in the balance sheet in order to avoid accounting for losses.

The direct fiscal implications for the government's budget from these costs of QT can also vary by country based on its institutional arrangement. In countries such as the UK, any central bank losses must be compensated for directly from the government's budget according to pre-set terms; this is a very tangible cost that not only aggravates fiscal pressures for the government, but also can put the central bank in the center of political discussions on the budget. In other countries, such as Sweden, the central bank must negotiate with the government on the size of a fiscal injection to recapitalize after losses, leading to difficult conversations and concerns if the injection is not deemed to be sufficient.[4] In yet other countries (such as the United States), the central bank is allowed to run negative equity and make up for any losses over time without requiring any immediate funding from the government (although no remittances are paid to the government until the losses are recouped).

To better understand these trade-offs around QE, and in particular the short- and longer-term costs, several examples from Cecchetti and Hilscher (2024) show the magnitude of the fiscal impact of large central bank balance sheets for the United Kingdom, the United States, and Switzerland. Beginning with the UK, figure 7.1 shows that during the low interest rate environment from 2009 to 2022, the BoE remitted profits to the UK Treasury from its asset holdings equal to 6 percent of GDP. As interest rates increased after 2021, the situation changed abruptly. As of early 2024, and using market forecasts for future rates, the BoE is expected to pass on (undiscounted) losses of almost 8 percent of GDP through 2071.[5] Although these profits and losses may largely balance out over time, the sudden shift in cash flow is a challenge for the government. More specifically, the UK government received an average remittance of 0.44 percent of UK GDP each year from 2014 through 2022, which then quickly reversed to a net payment of 1.4 percent of GDP in 2023. In a year of tight budgets and a focus on fiscal consolidation, this quickly puts the central bank in the unwanted position of being in the middle of a difficult political debate.

In the United States, the Federal Reserve's ability to defer any net losses on its balance sheet (and make up for this with profits in future years) moderates the political discourse about the costs of QE.[6] This accounting, however, could create challenges in a country if the future profits never materialized. This does not appear to be an issue in the United States, however, as the losses are expected to be short-lived and outweighed by profits over longer periods (even if not in every single year). More specifically, Cecchetti and Hilscher (2024) use data from Levin and Skinner (2024) to show that U.S. QE corresponded to net profits for the Federal Reserve in all years except from 2023 through 2025. The losses in 2023 are estimated to be meaningful (at 0.5 percent of GDP), but are forecast to be balanced by net profits over 2026–2040.

In contrast to the United States and the United Kingdom, where the costs of large central bank asset holdings are primarily determined by changes in interest rates and local currency bond valuations, in Switzerland (and many emerging markets) these costs also reflect fluctuations in the exchange rate. In fact, if a central bank owns FX-denominated assets in its portfolio, large currency movements can cause even larger swings in profits and losses from year to year than typically experienced from the interest rate carry and capital gains/losses. For example, figure 7.2 (from Cecchetti and Hilscher 2024)

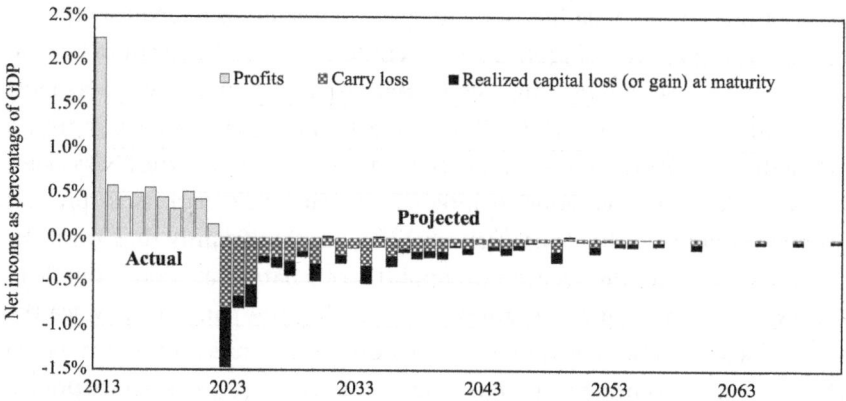

Figure 7.1
Bank of England: Net profits and losses from asset purchase facility, 2013–2071. *Note*: Data through 2023 are the net transfers from the Bank of England to the UK Treasury as reported by the UK Office of National Statistics. For 2023, the division between the carry loss and the capital loss is the estimate in Cecchetti and Hilscher (2024). Data for 2024 to 2071 are estimates in Cecchetti and Hilscher (2024) based on the information on the holdings of the BoE's Asset Purchase Facility, combined with a forward interest curve as published by the BoE, assuming that all bonds in the APF are held to maturity. Data for GDP through 2028 are from the IMF. From 2028 on, nominal GDP is assumed to grow at a 3.6 percent constant rate consistent with assumptions in the Office of Budget Responsibility (2023). *Source*: Replicated from figure 2 in Cecchetti and Hilscher (2024), which uses data from UK Office of National Statistics, Bank of England, IMF's World Economic Outlook database, and authors' calculations.

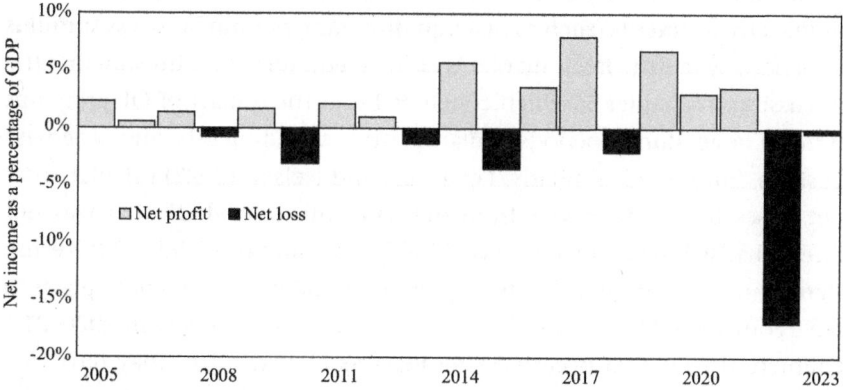

Figure 7.2
Swiss National Bank: Net income as percent of GDP: 2005–2023. *Note*: Swiss National Bank's net income as a percentage of nominal GDP. *Source*: Replicated from figure 5 in Cecchetti and Hilscher (2024). Underlying data from Swiss National Bank.

shows this extreme volatility for the Swiss National Bank (SNB)—with net income swinging from a profit of 8 percent to a loss of 17 percent of GDP in any given year (and reflecting a combination of exchange rate movements and valuation changes). The SNB's large asset holdings, however, reflect a different rationale than in most other advanced economies; the SNB's assets largely reflect past decisions to intervene in currency markets to prevent an overvaluation of the Swiss franc (which can significantly drag on inflation). This includes the decision to support an exchange rate floor from 2011 through 2015, as well as FX intervention during the pandemic.[7] Since the GFC, Switzerland has relied more heavily on this FX intervention instead of QE as its "unconventional" tool to support the economy and stabilize prices.[8]

Of course, in order to evaluate if these asset purchase programs are an optimal strategy, it is necessary to weigh their costs against their benefits (as well as incorporate other, harder to measure costs than those discussed earlier).[9] Asset purchase programs enacted during the periods of severe financial stress in 2008 and 2020 to keep markets functioning undoubtedly yielded substantial benefits; it is impossible to guess at the cost of a complete financial collapse that might have occurred without these policy responses. QE programs that reduce borrowing costs and support growth and price stability also yield benefits over time.

Although capturing these aggregate macroeconomic effects is challenging, recent research suggests that the relative costs and benefits can change based on the economic environment. For example, Adrian et al. (2024) show that QE provides a large boost to aggregate demand in stressed economic environments (such as in a liquidity trap), but provides less stimulus in periods when the labor market is close to equilibrium. This supports the discussion in chapter 5, which concluded that the impact of QE programs is much larger during periods of market stress and illiquidity, and otherwise positive, but muted. Similarly, Levin, Lu, and Nelson (2022) calculate that net losses to U.S. taxpayers from the pandemic-related QE that was not directed at stabilizing markets was $640 billion, and this "did not have any significant effect in reducing term premiums and hence does not appear to have contributed to the very rapid pace of economic recovery in 2020–21." Granted, the QE that occurred after markets had stabilized may have had hard-to measure benefits, such as improving consumer and business confidence and thereby strengthening the broader recovery. All in all, however, these results suggest that the asset purchases that occurred after markets had stabilized and as economies bounced back may have generated net costs, albeit with the benefit of hindsight and new insights on how the costs of large central bank balance sheets can evolve over time.[10]

Finally, just as insufficient attention to the costs of military conflict can hinder the ability of an army to maintain adequate supplies to fight effectively in the next battle, large central bank losses could generate challenges in terms of political backlash that then limits central banks' ability to maneuver in the future. While central banks received little credit when they passed on profits from QE in the decade before the pandemic, recent losses have garnered substantial attention (particularly in countries where the losses must be made up by the fiscal authority). In some countries, this has contributed to government decisions to limit the ability of central banks to use certain unconventional weapons in the future.[11] This more limited room to maneuver could complicate their ability to fight the next crisis.

Moreover, even if central banks maintain the ability to use most of their new tools, the costs discussed earlier could complicate more conventional interest rate decisions. For example, if raising interest rates to achieve an inflation mandate generates a large fiscal cost (due to the central bank's interest rate carry or capital losses on its bonds) or increases the risk of a sovereign debt crisis, how would that factor into a central bank's decision? This trade-off is particularly challenging for countries with large asset holdings—such as Japan. *The Economist* calculates that for every 0.25-percentage-point rise in the yields of Japanese bonds (across all maturities), the central bank's bond holdings will fall in value by about $58bn—about 1.5 percent of Japanese GDP.[12] In an extreme scenario, if these losses contribute to a financial crisis or spike in risk premiums, would this prevent a central bank from adjusting rates to achieve its price stability mandate?

While a full assessment of the trade-offs of the multifaceted tools used in response to the GFC and the pandemic is beyond the scope of this book, the experience of the last two decades highlights the importance of following Sun Tzu's advice of evaluating the costs as well as the benefits of different strategies—including the long-term ramifications. Although policymakers may be tempted to "do whatever it takes" during a crisis, they should still consider the trade-offs of different strategies. A greater awareness of the costs of asset purchases would likely not have prevented the use of QE, but may have caused it to be used more judiciously (especially after markets stabilized). Also, greater attention to these trade-offs could have spurred more debate about different ways to structure asset purchase programs in order to minimize the subsequent costs. As is the case in a military confrontation, it is important to consider not only each battle in isolation, but also how it impacts your ability to win the longer war.

Suggestions for Incorporating the Trade-Offs from Unconventional Policies

As central banks face the fiscal costs of unconventional policies enacted over the last two decades (albeit in different forms for different countries), it is an opportune time to consider if there are strategies that could reduce these costs in the future, without undermining the benefits and efficacy of the policies. The range of strategies and experiences in different countries provide several useful ideas to improve the trade-offs of using these new weapons in the future.

First, any use of unconventional tools should carefully evaluate both the potential costs and the potential benefits when designing the program. Granted, these can be challenging to quantify—especially when emergency intervention is believed to provide the benefit of avoiding a systemic financial collapse. Yet, even in these emergency situations, there can be different costs for similar strategies that all provide substantial support. Also, in periods when asset purchases are aimed at supporting growth and price stability (rather than addressing financial stress), central banks should provide analysis calibrating the scale and scope of asset purchases in order to meet their economic objectives. For example, the announcement of a new QE package should include a detailed analysis of how a given amount of purchases affects inflation and growth (based on past multipliers), and how this is expected to return inflation to the target in a fixed amount of time. These types of estimates are imprecise, but were largely missing from the QE programs announced around the pandemic. This lack of quantification may have contributed to QE programs that were larger and lasted longer than needed (as discussed in chapter 6), and may have generated larger costs than required to reach inflation targets.

Second, any asset purchase program should require careful consideration of the costs of holding the assets and unwinding the program. As discussed in detail in chapter 6, this entails considering the duration of assets when deciding what to purchase (as shorter-term assets will roll off more quickly).

This also entails consideration of exactly which types of assets to include in the program. For example, including MBS provides more of a boost to the housing sector (which can be a valuable benefit if housing is contributing to systemic financial stress), but comes with a larger cost in terms of involving a slower roll-off of securities if interest rates increase.

A final suggestion is to carefully consider the institutional arrangement and accounting for the costs of these programs, not only to accurately assess the trade-offs, but also to distribute the gains and losses in a way that does not hinder the ability of central banks to accomplish their mandates in the future. More specifically, if assets held by a central bank lose value, they should be marked-to-market so that any large losses (or gains) are fully understood and surprises do not occur at a later date. This would also avoid incentivizing a central bank to avoid selling its assets (active QT) simply because it would force the bank to account for losses that have already occurred. If governments are ultimately responsible for losses or recapitalizing a central bank, or both, there should be a structure in which the government signs off on a major new asset purchase program, but then is responsible for indemnifying any net losses, in order to not to constrain the ability of the central bank to function effectively. In a true emergency, governments would be unlikely to block support, and by accepting responsibility a priori, this should reduce (albeit probably not stop) their criticism of any subsequent costs. In most cases, these types of arrangements must be decided by governments, and not central banks, which makes sense as the ultimate costs must be borne by the country and should be supported by elected officials.

8 Conclusion

The economic and financial upheaval over the last two decades has pushed governments and central banks to substantially expand their tools, authority, and reach. They have innovated and developed a new set of weapons and tactics to meet this series of unprecedented challenges. This experience has provided central banks with a number of important lessons about what works, what does not work, and what can be done better in the future. Many of these lessons resonate across time and across fields—including echoing the insights of the Chinese philosopher Sun Tzu.

An overarching insight from these lessons, as well as from Sun Tzu, is that the optimal strategy involves weighing multiple factors and then choosing a combination of tactics tailored to address the specific situation and environment. There is no "one-size-fits-all" solution. Monetary policy, like war, is more of an art than a science.

Nonetheless, the optimal combination of tactics (for monetary policy as well as war) should be based on six core principles: (1) planning in advance for the next battle; (2) accepting and adapting to the inevitability of powerful, external shocks outside your control; (3) establishing a strong tactical position; (4) developing a variety of weapons that you can combine for different maneuvers and situations; (5) maintaining flexibility so that you can quickly modify your strategy; and (6) considering the longer-term costs when evaluating the trade-offs of different approaches.[1] There is no single action, tactic, or equation that can guarantee victory in all environments, but this set of guiding principles can greatly increase the odds of accomplishing your goals.

These guiding principles, however, incorporate a tension. They emphasize the role of external factors—the "heaven" of Sun Tzu and the global shocks of central banks. Even the most powerful general, central bank governor, or head of state cannot stop or control these events. They often come as a surprise and can completely change the environment (or shape the outcome of a battle)—particularly today as the role of global shocks has increased over time. But then how much power does a policymaker or general actually have in the presence of these heavenly shocks? When growth and inflation around the world are highly synchronized—such as the widespread collapses around the GFC and the pandemic and subsequent spike in inflation—do the actions of individual central banks make a meaningful difference?

The answer is a resounding yes. Although central banks cannot stop these global shocks or avoid their initial detonation, they can mitigate the impact and support faster and longer-lasting recoveries. They can help build more resilient economies that are not only better defended against these shocks, but that sustain stronger growth across the decades after the effects of these shocks fade.

To make this point, I will end with some figures that quickly convey a substantial amount of information and highlight the importance of domestic policy decisions in a world of powerful global shocks and interconnected financial markets. (In this book, the figures are in black and white, but in the lecture behind this book and original CEPR working paper version, the figures are in a much more dramatic and informative color palette.) Each cell in these heat maps shows the correlation between the two countries listed on the horizontal and vertical axes, meaning that it shows how synchronized two countries are (for the given variable). Instead of reporting a precise number for each correlation, the cells are shaded using the distribution shown in the middle. Darker shades denote high correlations (i.e., a "hot" heat map) in which countries are highly synchronized, and the medium gray shades denote minimal comovement (i.e., a "cool" heat map). The cells on the 45-degree line are black (100 percent correlation) as this captures the perfect synchronization of each country with itself. Countries are also grouped by region, with the Euro area closer to the origin, emerging markets at the top and far right, and the non-Euro advanced economies in the middle.

To begin, figure 8.1 shows these heat maps for weekly correlations in equity returns.[2] Equity returns are a useful place to start as they should incorporate all available information on the expected future profitability of companies in a country, therefore capturing expected changes in real indicators. The panel on the top left shows these correlations from

1985 through 1995. The top row is almost all a very light gray, indicating basically no correlation between returns in Venezuela's stock market (the country for this top row) with that in other countries. A few cells in the bottom left are more medium gray—such as the cell for Canada and the United States—showing a more synchronized market between these neighbors (as expected). The point of these graphs, however, is not to focus on the details of any individual row or cell, but instead to capture broad trends in the overall shading over time. Viewed from this lens, 1985–1995 is very "cool"—with lots of light gray indicating very little synchronization between most countries' equity returns over this period, especially for the emerging markets around the edges.

The next graph in figure 8.1 shows these relationships over 2000–2007. This is a "warmer" heat map; there is less light gray and somewhat more medium and darker gray shades scattered throughout, especially in the bottom-left block for countries in the Euro area. This indicates increased synchronization in equity markets before the GFC. This is not surprising as this was the era of "hyper-globalization" after China entered the WTO, when trade increased rapidly, and supply chains around the world were restructured to link economies more tightly. It is also not surprising that this measure of integration increased even more quickly for members of the

Figure 8.1 *(next facing page)*
Weekly correlations in equity markets. *Note*: Each box is the average correlation in equity market returns between the countries listed on the horizontal and vertical axes over the period listed at the top. Darker shades are higher correlations. Equity returns are calculated as the weekly percent change in a broad market index in local currency. The index for Argentina is in U.S. dollars Countries included in the Euro area are Austria (AT), Belgium (BE), France (FR), Germany (DE), Greece (GR), Ireland (IE), Italy (IT), Luxembourg (LU), Portugal (PT), and Spain (ES). Countries included in Other AEs (i.e., Other Advanced Economies) are Australia (AU), Canada (CA), Czech Republic (CZ), Denmark (DK), Israel (IL), Japan (JP), Korea (KR), New Zealand (NZ), Norway (NO), Singapore (SG), Sweden (SE), Switzerland (CH), United Kingdom (UK), and United States (US). Countries included as EMEs (Emerging Market Economies) are Argentina (AR), Brazil (BR), Chile (CL), China (CN), Colombia (CO), Hungary (HU), India (IN), Indonesia (ID), Malaysia (MY), Mexico (MX), Pakistan (PK), Peru (PE), Philippines (PH), Poland (PL), Rusia (RU), South Africa (ZA), Thailand (TH), Turkey (TR), and Venezuela (VE). *Source*: Underlying data used to calculate the returns is from Datastream.

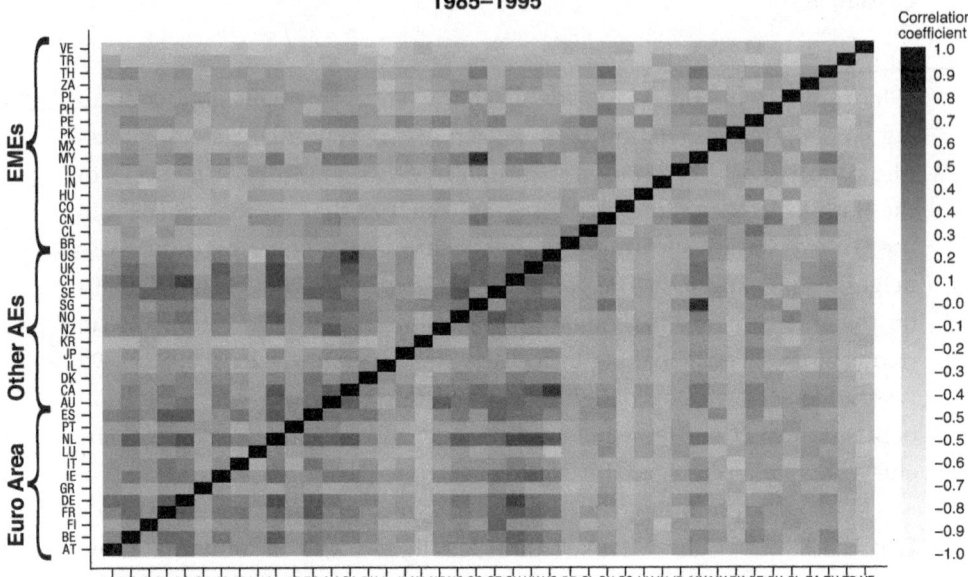

1985–1995

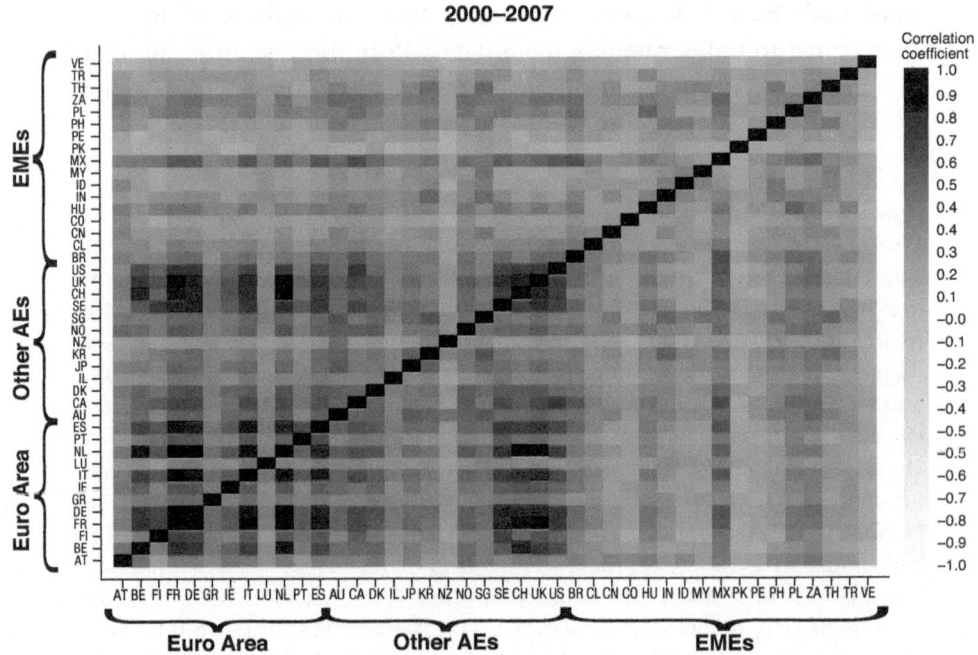

2000–2007

Figure 8.1

2008–2010

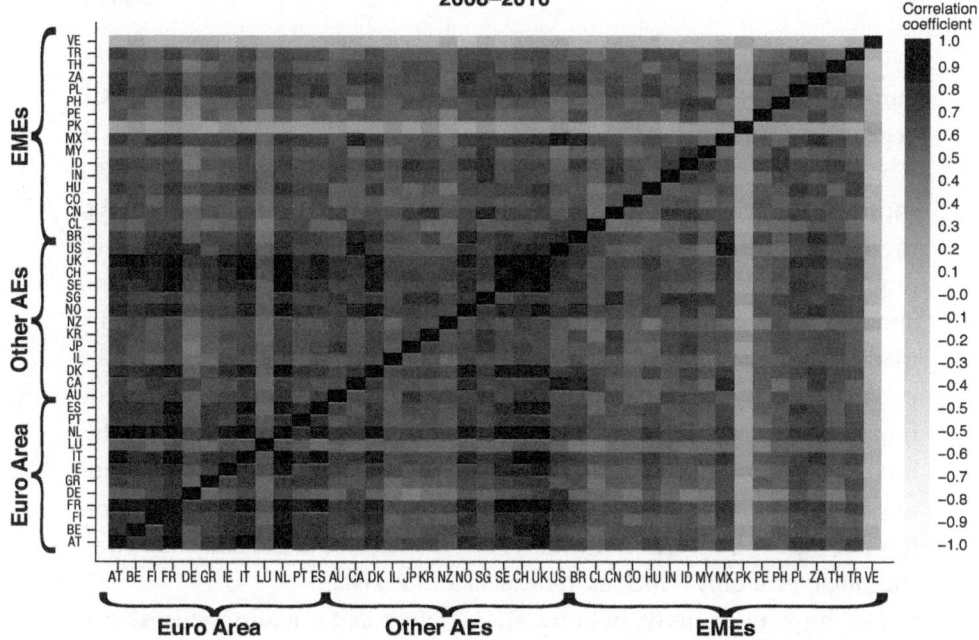

2020–2022

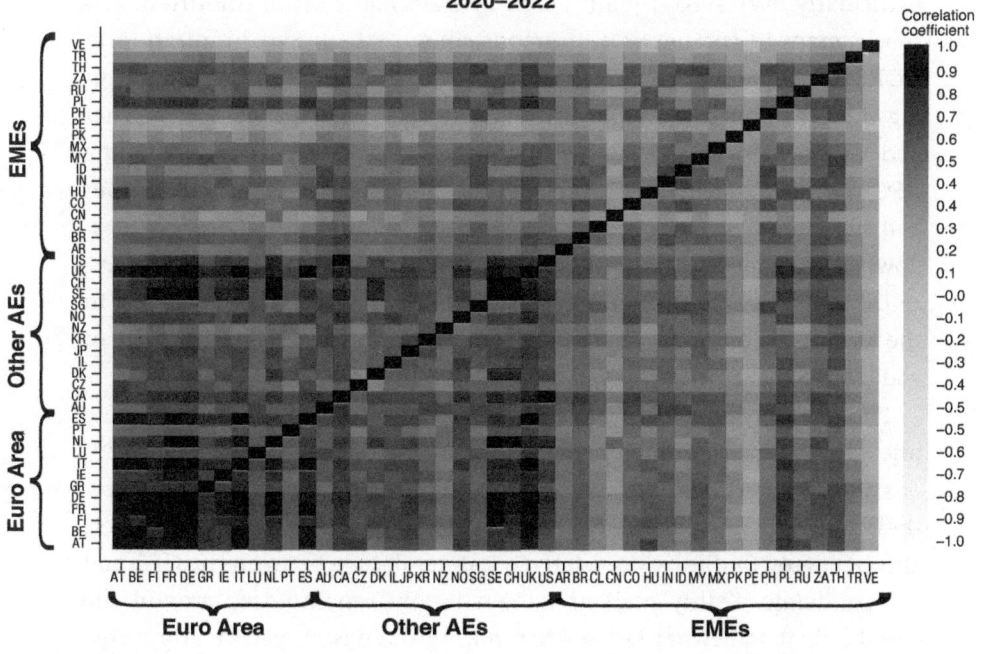

Figure 8.1
(continued)

Euro area, as 1999 was the start of the common currency and when the ECB began to set interest rates for the group.

Continuing to travel through time, the next set of panels in figure 8.1 shows the same correlations during the major crises of the last two decades: the GFC (2008–2010) and the pandemic (2020–2022). It is as if we just jumped to much bloodier battlefields. The graphs are very "hot" and almost entirely dark gray or black—even for most emerging markets. Equity markets around the world crashed and then rebounded together over these periods. This tight comovement during crises is typical and captures the impact of shocks from heaven (as discussed in detail in chapter 3). This increased synchronization also reflects a statistical effect that correlations mechanically increase during periods of heightened volatility.[3] The few lines of lighter gray are countries whose markets are less tightly linked to the global economy—such as Venezuela and Pakistan.

Do the same patterns hold for GDP growth as for equity returns? Figure 8.2 shows the same bilateral correlations for the same periods, except now focuses on comovements in GDP growth.[4] Data is more limited— particularly over 1985–1995 (as seen by the smaller set of countries). The "cool" maps in the next set of graphs show that the synchronization in GDP growth over 1985–1995 and 2000–2007 is fairly low, including during the period of hyper-globalization. The very "hot" panels for the later periods, however, show that this comovement increased sharply during the GFC and the pandemic. This captures the synchronized collapse in output and subsequent sharp rebounds—particularly around the COVID-19 lockdowns and reopenings. This was an extremely bloody shock from heaven.

Do these very "hot" maps suggest that policymakers have little power in the face of major global shocks? Is growth simply determined by "acts of god" that affect all countries simultaneously?

Policymakers should not lose heart. Even more important than these brief windows around major shocks is what happens over the longer periods after the effects of the shocks fade. To understand what happens over these longer periods, figure 8.3 shows the comovement in equity markets and GDP growth during the relatively calmer decade between the GFC and the pandemic. Equity markets remain highly synchronized around the world (albeit somewhat less so than during the crises), particularly across advanced economies. In contrast, GDP growth is much more independent. In other words, the high degree of synchronization in financial markets does not correspond to a high degree of synchronization in growth rates—except during major crisis periods. This is particularly striking as this relatively "calm" period in the 2010s that coincided with low comovement in growth rates was far from peaceful; it included the Euro crisis, a sharp slowdown in China and collapse in commodity prices, Brexit, and the start of a tariff war between the world's largest economies.

This series of results highlights why sound policy choices are still critically important in a world buffeted by large, external shocks. Yes—global shocks are powerful and will cause sharp swings in incomes, financial markets, inflation, and the broader economy. Policymakers cannot stop these heavenly shocks or their immediate effects on markets and growth. Financial markets also remain highly synchronized after the immediate effects of these shocks fade. But this is not true for growth rates. Instead, GDP growth is primarily determined by domestic factors, including domestic decisions by central banks and governments. In fact, it is quite striking that despite high levels of global integration through trade and capital flows, and despite the large and growing role of global shocks on a range of macroeconomic variables (chapter 3), GDP growth rates still march at their own national beat. Moreover, the evolution of GDP growth and income is a better metric to evaluate a nation's success than the performance of financial markets.[5] Domestic policy decisions—not external shocks—are more

Figure 8.2 *(next facing page)*
Correlations in GDP growth. *Note*: Each box is the average correlation in GDP growth between the countries listed on the horizontal and vertical axes over the period listed at the top. GDP growth is calculated on a quarterly basis using real, seasonally adjusted GDP. Darker shades are higher correlations. Countries included in the Euro area are Austria (AT), Belgium (BE), France (FR), Germany (DE), Greece (GR), Ireland (IE), Italy (IT), Luxembourg (LU), Portugal (PT), and Spain (ES). Countries included in Other AEs (Advanced Economies) are Australia (AU), Canada (CA), Czech Republic (CZ), Denmark (DK), Israel (IL), Japan (JP), Korea (KR), New Zealand (NZ), Norway (NO), Singapore (SG), Sweden (SE), Switzerland (CH), United Kingdom (UK), and United States (US). Countries included as EMEs (Emerging Market Economies) are Argentina (AR), Brazil (BR), Chile (CL), Colombia (CO), Hungary (HU), India (IN), Indonesia (ID), Mexico (MX), Philippines (PH), Poland (PL), South Africa (ZA), Thailand (TH), and Turkey (TR). *Source*: Underlying GDP data used to calculate growth rates is from the IMF's *International Financial Statistics*, accessed October 2024.

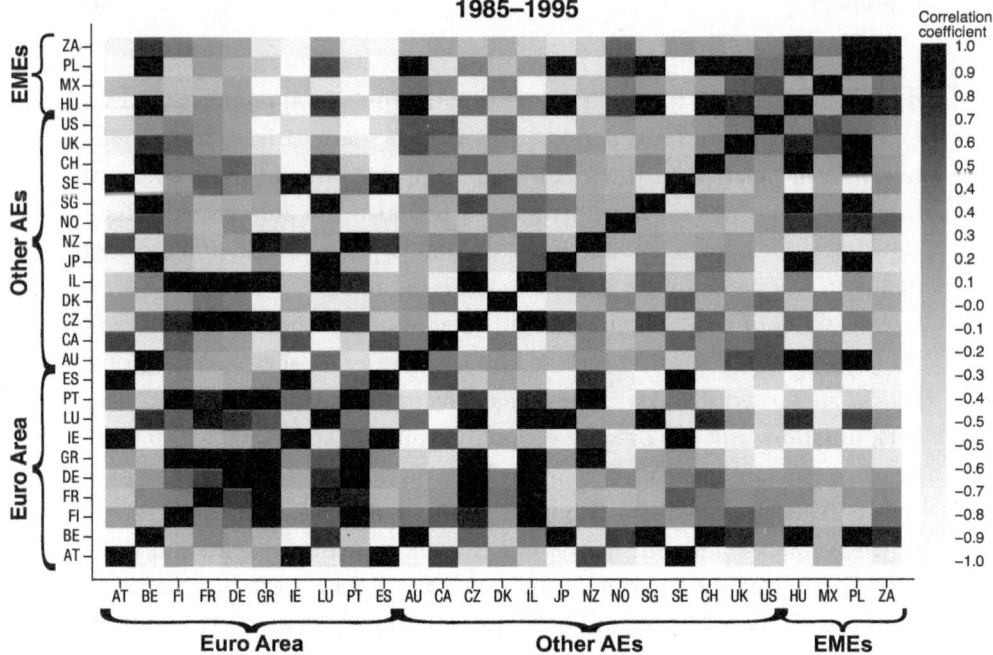

1985–1995

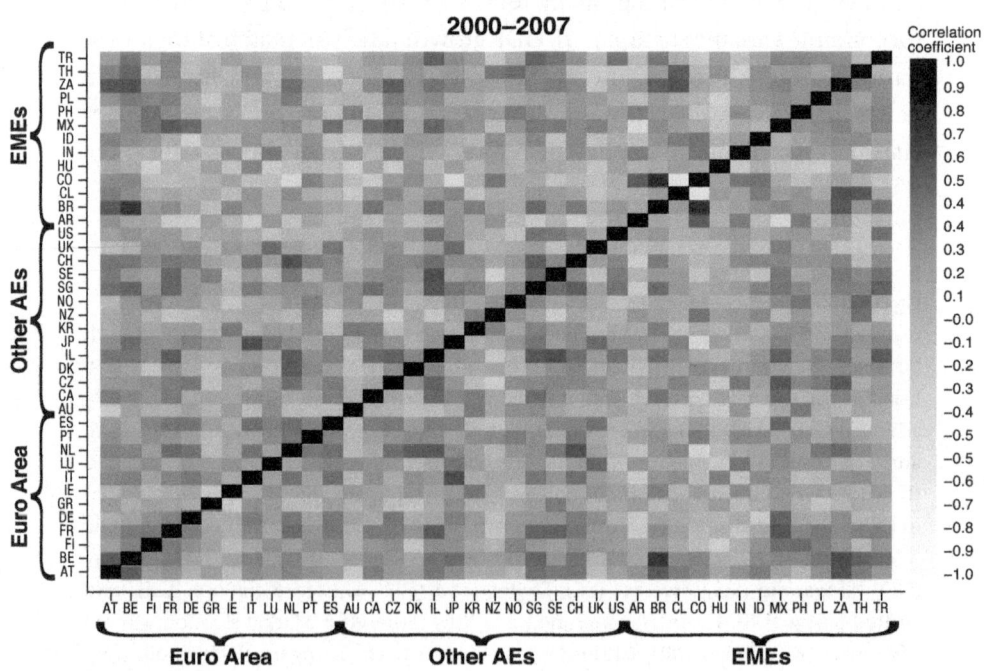

2000–2007

Figure 8.2

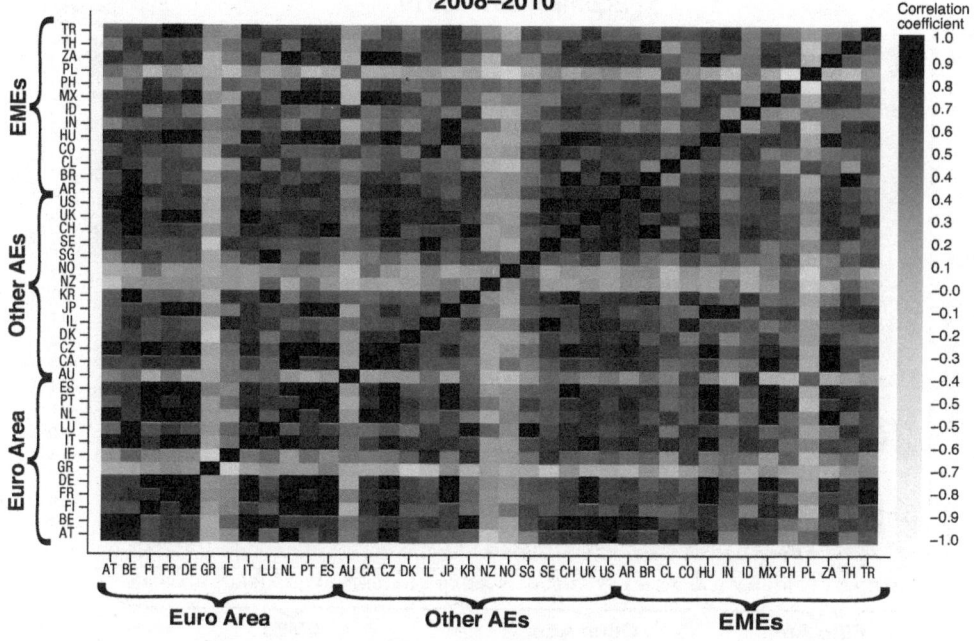

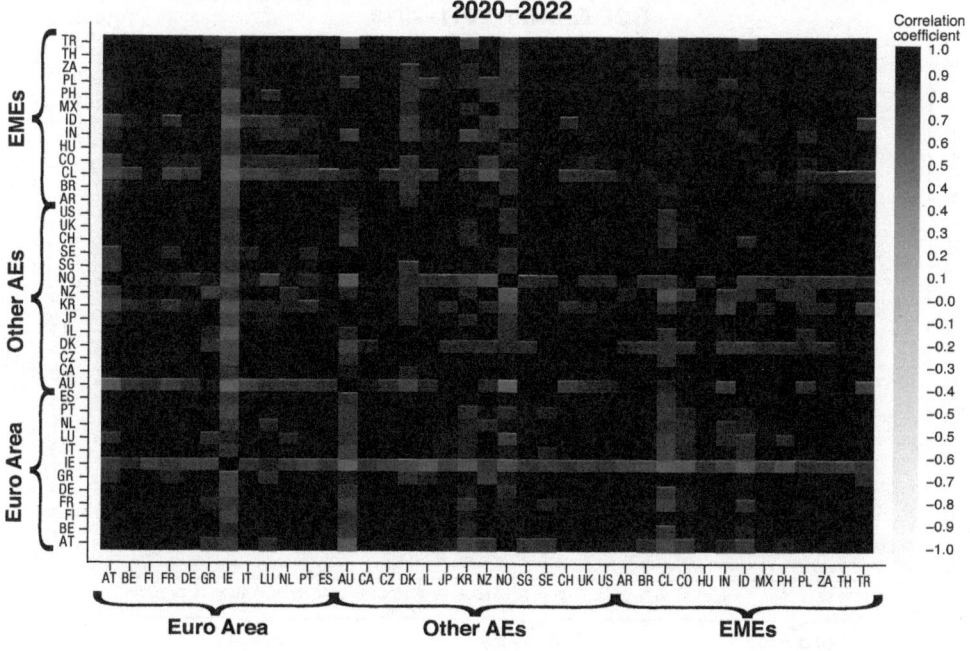

Figure 8.2
(continued)

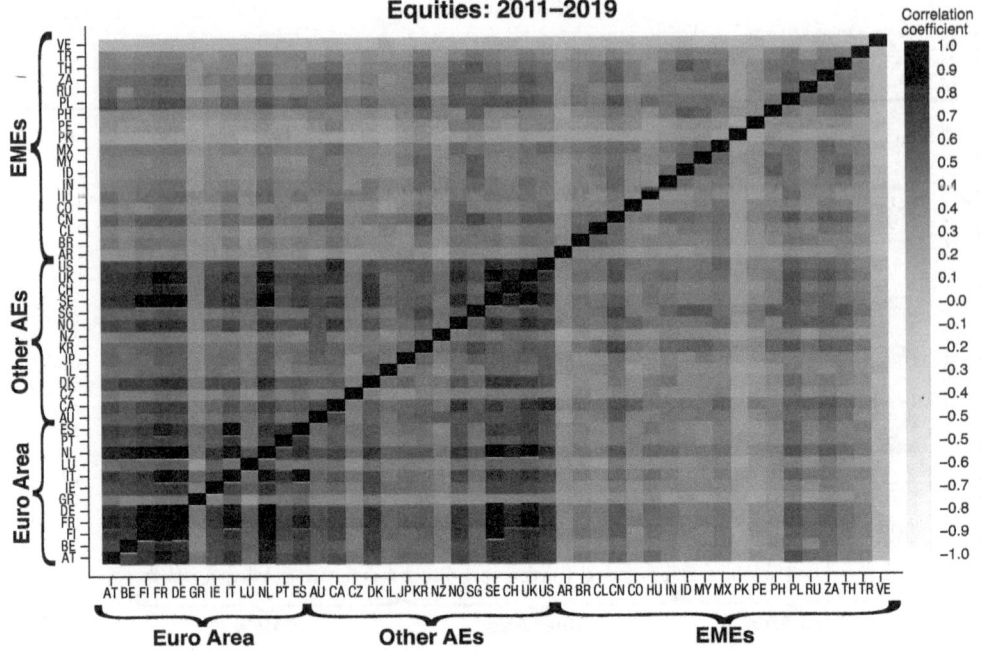

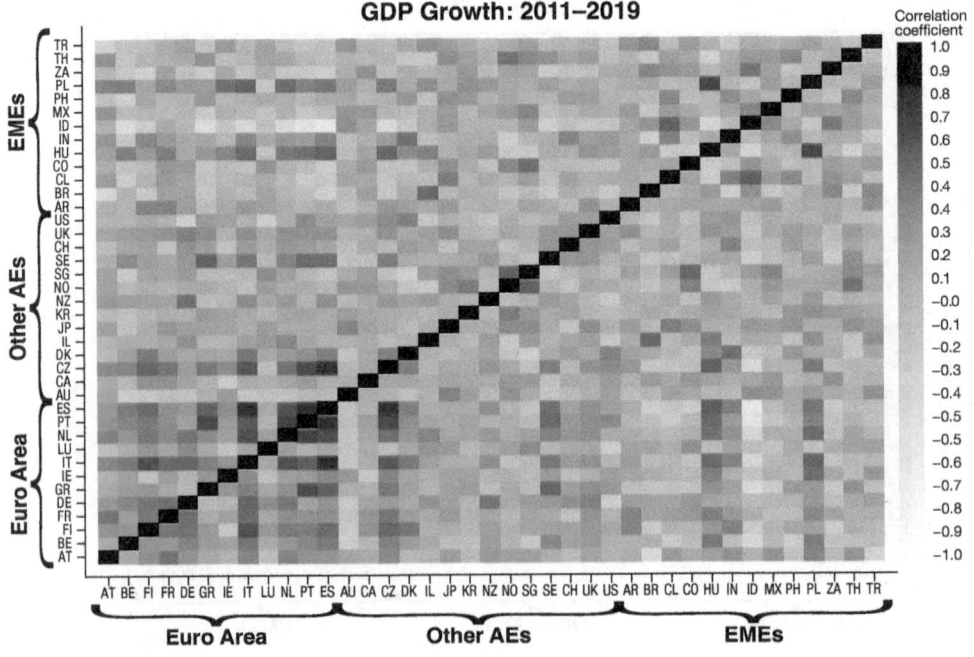

Figure 8.3
Correlations in equity markets vs. GDP growth: 2011–2019. *Note*: See notes to figures 8.1 and 8.2. Darker shades are higher correlations. *Source*: Underlying data on equities is from Datastream and for GDP is from the IMF. See notes to figures 8.1 and 8.2.

important in determining how this key measure of success evolves over long periods of time.

To conclude, Sun Tzu ends his first chapter highlighting the importance of sound decision making:

> The general that hearkens to my counsel and acts upon it, will conquer: let such a one be retained in command! The general that hearkens not to my counsel nor acts upon it, will suffer defeat:—let such a one be—dismissed! (Sun Tzu, *The Art of War*, Chapter 1, Principle 15)

Even in a world of powerful external shocks from heaven, policy choices matter. Following the principles outlined by Sun Tzu and discussed in this book will allow central banks to retain their command and continue to support their economies so that they are ready for the next war.

Acknowledgments

Thanks to the Swiss National Bank and ETH Zurich for inviting me to present the Karl Brunner Distinguished Lecture on October 3, 2024, in Zurich, and particularly to Chairman Martin Schlegel and former Chairman Thomas Jordan. For further information on this lecture series, see https://www.snb.ch/en/services-events/events/karl-brunner-lectures#. Thanks to my coauthors who contributed to the discussions and research underlying many themes in this lecture: Katharina Bergant, Anusha Chari, Karlye Dilts-Stedman, Wenxin Du, Bill English, Christian Friedrich, Jongrim Ha, Ayhan Kose, Matthew Luzzetti, Dennis Reinhardt, and Ángel Ubide. Further thanks to Chris Collins and Jose Ignacio Llodra for assistance preparing these remarks and to Viral Acharya, Stephen Cecchetti, Karlye Dilts-Stedman, Wenxin Du, and Bill English for detailed comments on earlier drafts. All views in this lecture are my own and do not necessarily reflect those of my coauthors or any institutions with which I am affiliated.

Notes

Chapter 1

1. Sun Tzu was a military general who lived in China around 544–496 BC. He is best known for his volume *The Art of War*. These principles and his philosophy have been applied to range of fields well outside of the military—including running a business, legal strategies, competing in sports, and codes of conduct for personal life.

2. Sun Tzu includes many other principles that could be useful to central banks—but they will be saved for a future discussion. For example, he highlights the importance of collecting information from a variety of sources (including the varied uses of spies), as well as tenets for effective leadership.

3. The data used to calculate these growth rates is from the Maddison Project Database (2023). The "full sample" in the figure is the fifty-eight countries from the full dataset with GDP data for both 1950 and 2022. "Advanced economies" is a subset of the twenty-four countries defined as advanced by the IMF in 2022 and used later in this book.

Chapter 2

1. It is important to clarify that "crisis" does not mean a sharp movement in financial markets or bankruptcy in a major financial institution. Financial losses and corporate insolvencies are part of a healthy economy and efficient markets. Although these types of adjustments can be painful, they should not merit central bank intervention unless they threaten the functioning of the broader financial system.

2. For example, see Brunnermeier et al. (2016), Farhi and Tirole (2018), and Forbes (2013).

3. See Rose (2023) and Acharya, Gopel, et al. (2024) for more details on these recent banking crises.

4. Rose (2023).

5. Rose (2023). These outflow statistics include actual outflows over the first day of the run, plus outflows that were scheduled for the second day but did not occur because the banks were closed.

6. For an example of proposals based on the characteristics and vulnerabilities of Iceland, see Forbes (2018).

7. The Bank of England is an example of a central bank with this structure. It has three separate committees that focus on monetary policy, macroprudential policy, and prudential policy. Each committee includes a core of overlapping "internal" members, plus external members who serve only on one committee.

8. See Angeloni et al. (2024), Lengwiler and Weder di Mauro (2023), and Eggen et al. (2023).

9. For example, see *Key Attributes of Effective Resolution Regimes for Financial Institutions* (FSB 2024b) and *Stabilising Financial Markets: Lending and Market Making as Last Resort* (ESRB 2023).

Chapter 3

1. Data is from the IMF's World Economic Outlook database (April 2024), with reported data through 2023 and forecasts for 2024 and 2025. GDP data is the annual growth in gross domestic product in constant prices. CPI inflation is average annual consumer price inflation.

2. Figures 3.4 and 3.5 use the same data, definitions, and sample of advanced economies as figures 3.2 and 3.3.

3. To be in a tightening or easing phase, the central bank does not need to be adjusting monetary policy each meeting. See Forbes, Ha, and Kose (2024b) for details on how these tightening and easing phases are defined and the specific dates for each economy.

4. The exception is Japan, the only country where inflation remained "too cool" during this period.

5. For this analysis, interest rates are measured using the shadow interest rate from Krippner (2013), and if not available, the overnight rate or three-month yield. Inflation is measured as headline CPI inflation and growth as the growth of industrial production (as GDP growth is less widely available on a monthly basis, particularly earlier in the sample).

6. These graphs show the average percent variation in interest rates, inflation, and growth explained by these global and domestic shocks for thirteen advanced economies using the methodology and data from Forbes, Ha, and Kose (2024b), but for a larger set of economies. Forbes, Ha, and Kose (2024b) included five economies:

Canada (CAN), the Euro area (EA), Japan (JPN), United Kingdom (UK), and United States (USA). This discussion and figure 7 also include Australia (AUS), Switzerland (CHE), Denmark (DNK), Israel (ISR), South Korea (KOR), Norway (NOR), New Zealand (NZL) and Sweden (SWE).

7. The noteworthy exception is the outsized role of global shocks behind inflation over the period 1970–1984, although this partially reflects a smaller sample size and very high inflation in a few economies.

8. See Bandera et al. (2023) for additional discussion of how the optimal monetary policy response will vary based on the nature of the shock and the characteristics of the economy.

9. For more detailed discussion and evidence, see Forbes (2020) and Ha, Kose, and Ohnsorge (2019).

10. Recent work shows that even though tariffs, geopolitics, and other restrictions have affected trade and capital flows, much of this reflects changes in the patterns of bilateral flows rather than decreases in overall integration. For example, although trade between the United States and China has fallen sharply since the escalation in tariffs starting in 2017, a portion of this trade has been rerouted through other economies (particularly in Asia), similar to adding additional depots in a military supply chain. For additional discussion, see Gopinath et al. (2024), Setser (2024), and Strain (2024).

11. Granted, focusing on a single number instead of a range is easier to communicate and may therefore be more effective at anchoring expectations, but it could be possible to focus on a single number that is the midpoint of a range in general communication (i.e., return inflation to "around X"), backed by a range around X in more technical discussions.

12. See Forbes (2020) for more discussion. For a recent prominent example, see Hooper, Mishkin, and Sufi (2019).

13. See Bandera et al. (2023) for discussion of how the characteristics of the shock and state of the economy determine the appropriate monetary policy response.

Chapter 4

1. See chapters 9 and 10 in Sun Tzu's *The Art of War*.

2. See Angeloni et al. (2024) for a thoughtful discussion of the progress made in macroprudential oversight, lessons from the banking collapses in 2023, and priorities for the next stage of reforms.

3. Macroprudential regulation encompasses a diverse set of tools focused on the stability of the entire financial system, including the buildup of systemic risk over

time, as well as how vulnerabilities in individual institutions can spillover or interact with other policies to affect the entire economy. Prudential (or microprudential) regulation focuses on the stability of individual financial institutions. There can be substantial overlap between prudential and macroprudential regulations, particularly in countries where the financial system is dominated by a small number of financial institutions).

4. See Forbes (2021) for more details on this work and the resulting progress.

5. This measure of the macroprudential stance is based on data from the International Monetary Fund's Integrated Macroprudential Policy (iMaPP) database, described in Alam et al. (2019). Forbes (2021) and Bergant and Forbes (2023a) calculate the net changes in macroprudential policy each year (with a +1 for a tightening of any macroprudential policy and a −1 for each loosening), and then cumulates these changes each year starting in 1990 (which is set at 0) to calculate the aggregate stance shown in the graph. Forbes (2021) and Chari, Dilts-Stedman, and Forbes (2022) also report an alternate measure of the macroprudential stance that accounts for the magnitudes of adjustments, but for a more limited set of tools, and shows similar patterns over time.

6. See Forbes (2021) for more evidence and details on the discussion that follows.

7. Major challenges in this empirical assessment include: measuring the intensity of macroprudential tools, reverse causality, omitted variable bias, limited time series available to date, and challenges capturing multifaceted spillovers and leakages.

8. For example, see Ostry et al. (2010) and Forbes et al. (2015).

9. For evidence, see Ahnert et al. (2021), Aiyar, Calomiris, and Wieladek (2014), and Akinci and Olmstead-Rumsey (2018).

10. Estimates of the magnitudes of these leakages vary across countries, regulations, and studies. For example, Aiyar, Calomiris, and Wieladek (2014) estimate that resident foreign branches fill in about one-third of the initial contraction in domestic lending from tighter regulations in the UK, while Ahnert et al. (2020) estimate that corporate debt issuance filled in for about 10 percent of the contraction in domestic lending from tighter foreign exchange requirements. Beirne and Friedrich (2017) show that there are larger leakages and spillovers in countries that have more developed NBFIs and that are more open to international banks.

11. Acharya, Carletti, et al. (2024) provide evidence of another important and hard-to-measure link between banks and NBFIs that has increased vulnerability—of bank credit lines to real estate investment trusts (which have substantial exposure to commercial real estate).

12. Hanson, Kashyap, and Stein (2011) and Cecchetti and Schoenholtz (2017) show that countercyclical buffers have not been set at optimal levels. Kashyap and Stein (2004) shows the benefits of using the countercyclical capital buffer.

Chapter 5

1. See Benford (2024).

2. A prominent example is the United States under Federal Reserve Chairman Paul Volcker from 1979 to 1982.

3. See Bernanke (2020) for an excellent discussion of this new toolkit.

4. For overviews of the multifaceted central bank responses to the 2008 global financial crisis, see CGFS (2019) for a cross-country analysis, Hartman and Smets (2018) for the Euro area, and Bernanke, Geithner, and Paulson (2019) for the United States.

5. For more details on these programs, see Bernanke, Geithner, and Paulson (2019) and Bernanke (2020).

6. For overviews of the QE programs adopted around the world, see Borio and Zabai (2016) and Gagnon and Sack (2018). Also see Fratto et al. (2021) for emerging markets, Hartman and Smets (2018) for the Euro area, and Krishnamurthy and Vissing-Jorgenson (2012) and Kuttner (2018) for the United States.

7. D'Amico and Kaminska (2019) find that the UK corporate bond purchase program reduced spreads for all types of bonds but had a greater impact on bonds eligible for the program. Krishnamurthy and Vissing-Jorgensen (2013) find a greater impact of QE on MBS and Treasury yields when each type of security is included in a QE program, with minimal spillovers to other asset classes.

8. See CGFS (2023) for details on central bank asset purchase programs in response to the pandemic.

9. The APP currently includes four components: the corporate sector purchase program (CSPP); the public sector purchase program (PSPP); the asset-backed securities purchase program (ABSPP), and the third covered bond purchase program (CBPP3).

10. Monetary policy decisions, europa.eu.

11. These statistics are from Bergant and Forbes (2023b) and based on the self-reported IMF Policy Tracker. As explained in this article, these likely underreport the use of FX intervention.

12. Results from Bergant and Forbes (2023a), based on data in Adler et al. (2021).

13. It is also worth noting one "unconventional" tool was not widely used—capital controls—despite efforts by institutions such as the International Monetary Fund to normalize and support their use. More specifically, Bergant and Forbes (2023b) report that in the first half of 2020, only 8 percent of emerging markets reduced controls on capital inflows (Peru, India, and China) and 5 percent tightened

controls on capital outflows (Turkey and Argentina). Only one advanced economy reported adjusting its capital flow measures (Korea, which reduced controls on capital inflows). The authors caution, however, that this is based on self-reported data from the IMF Tracker, which may understate adjustments in capital controls.

14. For evidence, see Borio and Zabai (2016) and Krishnamurthy and Vissing-Jorgensen (2012, 2013).

15. Sweden also announced plans to start QT in 2019, but those plans were derailed when the pandemic hit and Sweden restarted QE. Other central banks (such as the ECB) were able to shrink their balance sheets during certain windows, but this generally involved the expiration of past programs, rather than QT aimed at unwinding assets purchased as part of a QE program.

16. More specifically, Du, Forbes, and Luzzetti (2024) shows that securities holdings for the seven central banks in their sample fell from a peak of more than $8 trillion in mid-2022 by nearly $2.2 trillion through the end of 2023. They forecast an additional $2.2 trillion in reductions by the end of 2025 if central banks continued QT according to the parameters announced as of January 2024.

17. See Forbes (2022) for additional details on how QT can affect different segments of the yield curve, and thereby different sectors of the economy, as compared to increases in the policy interest rate.

18. For analysis of the impact of the U.S. QT from 2017 to 2019, see Smith and Valcarcel (2023).

19. The convenience yield is measured as the spread between the interest rate swap rate and the government bond yield of the same maturity (i.e., the swap spread). This reflects the premium that investors are willing to pay for the "convenience" of holding the government bond.

20. As discussed in detail in Du, Forbes, and Luzzetti (2024), the estimated effects are smaller in the United States as the Federal Reserve had extensive "preliminary discussions" about its plans for QT over several months before announcing the start of the program. As a result, much of the impact was not a surprise and thereby likely priced in before the announcement date that is the focus of the empirical analysis. D'Amico et al. (2012) show how adjusting for the surprise component can meaningfully increase the estimated effects of announcements of balance sheet policies.

21. See Bergant and Forbes (2023a) for a discussion of the use of macroprudential tools in response to the pandemic; see Hanson, Kashyap, and Stein (2011) for the calibration of these tools to have a meaningful countercyclical effect.

22. In 2019, the decline in reserve balances in the United States created liquidity strains in money markets.

Chapter 6

1. See English, Forbes, and Ubide (2024) for a much more extensive discussion of why inflation picked up faster than expected and why central banks were slow to respond, including in-depth case studies of the specific situations in major advanced economies and emerging markets. Also see Ha, Kose, and Ohnsorge (2021) for a detailed analysis of why inflation accelerated faster than expected.

2. The exceptions were Norway, New Zealand, and the UK, each of which started raising rates by the end of 2021.

3. These graphs show the median values for all economies with available data. Each variable is measured as the percent change (or change) relative to a year earlier (to eliminate seasonality). The sample includes twenty-four advanced economies, with countries in the Euro area included as individual countries before 1999, and then as one economy for any phases beginning from 1999 onward (when the Euro area came into existence). See Forbes, Ha, and Kose (2024b) for more details.

4. Although the United States did not experience a recession or even sharp deceleration in activity, this largely reflected the substantial fiscal stimulus that continued to support activity.

5. As noted in earlier in the book, the Phillips curve is the correlation between unemployment and inflation. Since 2008, reductions in unemployment corresponded to a weak pickup in wages and inflation, suggesting the relationship between these variables was weak (i.e., flat). Forbes, Gagnon, and Collins (2022), however, show that the Phillips curve is nonlinear, such that the impact of changes in unemployment on inflation is low when unemployment is high (i.e., the curve is flat), but becomes large and significant when unemployment is low (i.e., the curve becomes steep).

6. See English and Sack (2024) for an excellent discussion of details of how this applied to the U.S. experience.

7. In addition to the more general constraints discussed in this paragraph, some central banks also had idiosyncratic concerns. For example, the Federal Reserve had a new mandate that focused more on full employment and made it harder to act pre-emptively in response to inflation (Romer and Romer 2024). The ECB worried about the impact on spreads for countries with weaker fiscal positions, and the Riksbank was concerned about the impact on Sweden's households with high levels of debt linked to floating interest rates. See English, Forbes, and Úbide (2024) for more details.

8. The Reserve Bank of Australia implemented yield curve control by committing to buy government bonds in order to maintain the three-year government bond yield close to target (initially set at 0.25 percent and then reduced to 0.1 percent).

9. For evidence of this signaling effect of QE, see Krishnamurthy and Vissing-Jorgensen (2012, 2013), Bauer and Rudebusch (2014), and Bhattarai, Eggertsson, and Gafarov (2015).

10. The automatic trigger had an opt-out clause that QT would only occur "if appropriate given economic circumstances." See the BoE's *Monetary Policy Report* from August 2021, box A, for more details. The thresholds set after the pandemic were lower than those announced in earlier meetings, as the previous thresholds to start QT were never met.

11. The "taper tantrum" occurred in 2013 when Federal Reserve Chairman Bernanke hinted at the end to QE, triggering a sharp market reaction.

12. For example, see CIBC Weekly Roundup—May 28, 2021 (cibcassetmanagement .com).

13. See Du, Forbes, and Luzzetti (2024) for evidence on the different effects of active and passive QT.

14. More specifically, the BoC reduced its holdings of government bonds by 29 percent from the peak through the end of 2023, while the BoE reduced its holdings by only 13 percent. See Du, Forbes, and Luzzetti (2024) for more details on these balance sheet adjustments.

Chapter 7

1. For a summary of many of these arguments around the costs and benefits of low interest rates, see Forbes (2015).

2. See BIS (2019) for a discussion of how large central bank balance sheets can affect market functioning. This is a larger concern in economies where the central bank holds a larger share of market capitalization, such as Sweden and Japan.

3. In contrast, central banks often make profits when selling assets purchased as part of emergency liquidity and market support facilities, as these were often purchased at distressed prices and valuations recover after financial conditions normalize.

4. More specifically, the Riksbank must negotiate with the government after large losses on its asset holdings in order to receive capital injections to restore equity levels. In April 2024, the Riksbank asked for a capital injection of Skr 43.7 billion, but only received Skr 25 billion in September 2024. This has led to difficult discussions on how to treat the corresponding shortfall.

5. The calculations in this graph assume no gilt sales, such that the losses are the negative carry and loss at maturity with run-off. When the BoE sells UK Treasury bonds, they shift the losses to the present. The active bond sales that have occurred to date have meaningfully contributed to the cost for the BoE. Cecchetti and Hilscher (2024) calculate that average losses without active sales would have been 0.35 percent of GDP per year, as compared to 0.78 percent per year for the current program.

6. See English and Kohn (2022) for an excellent discussion of related issues for the U.S. Federal Reserve.

7. More specifically, in order to support the exchange rate floor, the SNB's FX reserves increased from 44 percent of GDP in 2011 to 76 percent in 2015. The SNB also intervened in FX markets during the pandemic, causing its reserve holdings to increase further to 125 percent of GDP in 2022.

8. See Jordan (2021) for an excellent discussion of the SNB's approach for using different conventional and unconventional tools.

9. For example, these costs could include less efficient market pricing and exposure to individual companies that could have idiosyncratic challenges (and even become insolvent). Hooley et al. (2023) provide a detailed discussion of a broader set of potential costs from the multifaceted programs aimed at supporting liquidity and market functioning during the GFC and the pandemic. This includes consideration of the broader set of financial exposures and liabilities as central banks and governments extended credit, subsidies, and indemnities to a range of counterparties for a variety of transactions. Accounting for potential losses is extremely challenging—and varies meaningfully across countries—but the losses could be much larger than the narrower set of losses discussed here.

10. Also see Greenlaw et al. (2018) for a skeptical view that QE provided a lasting and meaningful impact on bond yields or the economy as a whole.

11. For example, in January 2021 the U.S. Congress passed a law ending some of the pandemic-related support and restricting the use of the Exchange Stabilization Fund to fund certain types of programs in the future.

12. "Quantitative Easing Cost Hundreds of Billions. Was It Worth It?," *Economist*, July 23, 2023, https://www.economist.com/leaders/2023/07/31/quantitative-easing-cost-hundreds-of-billions-was-it-worth-it.

Chapter 8

1. Sun Tzu includes many other principles that would be useful to central banks—but those will be saved for a future discussion. For example, he includes extensive discussion about the importance of collecting information from a variety of sources, as well as tenets for effective leadership.

2. Equity returns are calculated as the percent change in the local currency index on a weekly basis. The indices are the broadest equity benchmark available for each country in Datastream.

3. See Forbes and Rigobon (2002) for a detailed explanation and examples of how heightened volatility during crises increases correlation coefficients, as well as suggestions for measuring this statistical effect.

4. GDP growth is calculated using real, quarterly, seasonally adjusted data from the IMF's *International Financial Statistics*.

5. Although no single variable can capture the wellbeing of a society (a measure that would need to incorporate considerations such as health outcomes, inequality, crime, environmental degradation, and more) GDP growth is a good proxy for the evolution of income and living standards for the entire population. It is also available at a quarterly basis over a long period of time for a large cross-section of countries, as required to estimate the heat maps.

References

Acharya, Viral, Elena Carletti, Fernando Restoy, and Xavier Vives. 2024. *Banking Turmoil and Regulatory Reform*. CEPR Press. https://www.iese.edu/media/research/pdfs/77782.

Acharya, Viral, Manasa Gopel, Maximilian Jager, and Sascha Steffen. 2024. "Shadow Always Touches the Feet: Implications of Bank Credit Lines to Non-Bank Financial Intermediaries." May 29. http://dx.doi.org/10.2139/ssrn.4847858.

Adler, Gustavo, Kyun Suk Chang, Rui Mano, and Yuting Shao. 2021. *Foreign Exchange Intervention: A Dataset of Public Data and Proxies*. IMF Working Paper WP/21/47.

Adrian, Tobias, Christopher Erceg, Marcin Kolasa, Jesper Lindé, Roger McLeod, Romain Veyrune, and Pawel Zabczyk. 2024. *Foreign Exchange Intervention: A Dataset of Public Data and Proxies*. IMF Working Paper WP/24/103.

Ahnert, Toni, Kristin Forbes, Christian Friedrich, and Dennis Reinhardt. 2021. "Macroprudential FX Regulations: Shifting the Snowbanks of FX Vulnerability." *Journal of Financial Economics* 140 (1): 145–174.

Aiyar, Shekhar, Charles Calomiris, and Tomasz Wieladek. 2014. "Does Macro-Pru Leak? Evidence from a UK Policy Experiment." *Journal of Money, Credit and Banking* 46 (1): 368–382.

Akinci, Ozge, and Jane Olmstead-Rumsey. 2018. "How Effective Are Macroprudential Policies? An Empirical Investigation." *Journal of Financial Intermediation* 33 (C): 33–57.

Alam, Zohair, Adrian Alter, Jesse Eiseman, Gaston Gelos, Heedon Kang, Machiko Narita, Erlend Nier, and Naixi Wang. 2019. *Digging Deeper—Evidence on the Effects of Macroprudential Policies from a New Database*. IMF Working Paper WP/19/66.

Angeloni, Ignazio, Stijn Claessens, Amit Seru, Sascha Stefen, and Beatrice Weder di Mauro. 2024. *Geneva 27: Much Money, Little Capital, and Few Reforms: The 2023 Banking Turmoil*. Paris and London: CEPR Press. https://cepr.org/publications/books-and-reports/geneva-27-much-money-little-capital-and-few-reforms-2023-banking.

Araujo, Juliana, Manasa Patnam, Adina Popescu, Fabien Valencia, and Weijia Yao. 2020. *Effects of Macroprudential Policy: Evidence from over 6,000 Estimates.* IMF Working Paper WP/20/67.

Avdjiev, Stefan, Cathérine Koch, Patrick McGuire, and Goetz von Peter. 2017. "International Prudential Policy Spillovers: A Global Perspective." *International Journal of Central Banking* 13: 5–37.

Bailey, Andrew, Jonathan Bridges, Richard Harrison, Josh Jones, and Aakash Mankodi. 2020. *The Central Bank Balance Sheet as a Policy Tool: Past, Present and Future.* Bank of England Staff Working Paper 899. London: Bank of England.

Bandera, Nicolo, Lauren Barnes, Matthieu Chavaz, Silvana Tenreyro, and Lukas von dem Berge. 2023. *Monetary Policy in the Face of Supply Shocks: The Role of Inflation Expectations.* Sintra ECB Forum Working Papers. https://www.ecb.europa.eu/press/conferences/ecbforum/shared/pdf/2023/Tenreyro_paper.pdf.

Bauer, Michael, and Glenn Rudebusch. 2014. "The Signaling Channel for Federal Reserve Bond Purchases." *International Journal of Central Banking* 10 (3): 233–289.

Beirne, John, and Christian Friedrich. 2017. "Macroprudential Policies, Capital Flows, and the Structure of the Banking Sector." *Journal of International Money and Finance* 75 (C): 47–68.

Benford, James. 2024. "A Weathervane for a Changing World: Refreshing Our Data and Analytics Strategy." Speech presented at Big Data and AI World at Tech Show London, March 7. https://www.bankofengland.co.uk/-/media/boe/files/speech/2024/march/a-weathervane-for-a-changing-world-speech-by-james-benford.pdf.

Bergant, Katharina, and Kristin Forbes. 2023a. "Macroprudential Policy during COVID: The Role of Policy Space." In *Macro-Financial Stability Policy in a Globalised World: Lessons from International Experience,* edited by Claudio Borio, Edward Robinson, and Hyun Song Shin. https://doi.org/10.1142/12921.

Bergant, Katharina, and Kristin Forbes. 2023b. "Policy Packages and Policy Space: Lessons from COVID-19." *European Economic Review* 158 (September). https://doi.org/10.1016/j.euroecorev.2023.104499.

Bergant, Katharina, Francesco Grigoli, Niels-Jakob Hansen, and Damiano Sandri. 2020. *Dampening Global Financial Shocks: Can Macroprudential Regulation Help (More than Capital Controls)?* IMF Working Paper WP/20/106. Washington, DC: International Monetary Fund.

Bernanke, Ben. 2020. "The New Tools of Monetary Policy." *American Economic Review* 110 (4): 943–983.

Bernanke, Ben, Tim Geithner, and Henry Paulson. 2019. *Firefighting: The Financial Crisis and Its Lessons.* New York: Penguin.

Bhattarai, Saroj, Gauti Eggertsson, and Bulat Gafarov. 2015. *Time Consistency and the Duration of Government Debt: A Signaling Theory of Quantitative Easing.* NBER Working Paper 21336. http://www.nber.org/papers/w21336.

BIS (Bank for International Settlements). 2019. *Large Central Bank Balance Sheets and Market Functioning.* Markets Committee, October. https://www.bis.org/publ/mktc11 .pdf.

Bolt, Jutta, and Jan Luiten van Zanden. 2024. "Maddison-Style Estimates of the Evolution of the World Economy: A New 2023 Update." *Journal of Economic Surveys* 39 (2): 631–671. https://doi.org/10.1111/joes.12618.

Boone, Laurence, and Lukasz Rawdanowicz. 2021. "Assessment of Monetary and Financial Policy Responses in Advanced Economies to the Covid-19 Crisis." In English, Forbes, and Ubide, eds., *Monetary Policy and Central Banking in the Covid Era,* 325–340.

Borio, Claudio, and Anna Zabai. 2016. *Unconventional Monetary Policies: A Reappraisal.* BIS Working Paper 570. https://www.bis.org/publ/work570.pdf.

Brunnermeier, Markus, Luis Garicano, Philip Lane, Marco Pagano, Ricardo Reis, Tano Santos, David Thesmar, Stijn Van Nieuwerburgh, and Dimitri Vayanos. 2016. "The Sovereign-Bank Diabolic Loop and ESBies." *American Economic Review, Papers and Proceedings* 106 (5): 501–512.

Buiter, Willem, Stephen Cecchetti, Kathryn Dominguez, and Antonio Sánchez-Serrano. 2023. *Stabilising Financial Markets: Lending and Market Making as Last Resort.* Reports of the Scientific Advisory Committee No. 13, January. European Systemic Risk Board (ESRB).

Cantú, Carlos, Paolo Cavallino, Fiorella De Fiore, and James Yetman. 2021. *A Global Database on Central Banks' Monetary Responses to Covid-19.* BIS Working Paper 934. https://www.bis.org/publ/work934.htm.

Cecchetti, Stephen, and Jens Hilscher. 2024. *Fiscal Consequences of Central Bank Losses.* NBER Working Paper 32478, May. https://www.nber.org/system/files/working _papers/w32478/w32478.pdf.

Cecchetti, Stephen G., and Kermit Schoenholtz. 2017. *Regulatory Reform: A Scorecard.* CEPR Discussion Paper DP12465.

CGFS (Committee on the Global Financial System). 2010. *Macroprudential Instruments and Frameworks: A Stocktaking of Issues and Experiences.* CGFS Papers No. 38. https://www.bis.org/publ/cgfs38.pdf.

CGFS (Committee on the Global Financial System). 2012. *Operationalizing the Selection and Application of Macroprudential Instruments.* CGFS Papers No. 48. https://www .bis.org/publ/cgfs48.pdf.

CGFS (Committee on the Global Financial System). 2019. *Unconventional Monetary Policy Tools: A Cross-Country Analysis.* CGFS Papers No. 63. https://www.bis.org/publ /cgfs63.pdf.

CGFS (Committee on the Global Financial System). 2023. *Central Bank Asset Purchases in Response to the Covid-19 Crisis.* CGFS Papers No. 68. https://www.bis.org /publ/cgfs68.pdf.

Chari, Anusha, Karlye Dilts-Stedman, and Kristin Forbes. 2022. "Spillovers at the Extremes: The Macroprudential Stance and Vulnerability to the Global Financial Cycle." *Journal of International Economics* 136 (C, May): 103582.

Claessens, Stijn. 2015. "An Overview of Macroprudential Tools." *Annual Review of Financial Economics* 7: 397–422.

D'Amico, Stefania, William B. English, David Lopez-Salido, and Edward Nelson. 2012. "The Federal Reserve's Large-scale Asset Purchase Programs: Rationale and Effects." *The Economic Journal* 122 (564): F415–F446.

D'Amico, Stefania, and Iryna Kaminska. 2019. *Credit Easing versus Quantitative Easing: Evidence from Corporate and Government Bond Purchase Programs.* Bank of England Staff Working Paper 825. https://www.bankofengland.co.uk/-/media/boe/files/working -paper/2019/credit-easing-versus-quantitative-easing-evidence-from-corporate-and -government-bond-purchase.pdf.

Du, Wenxin, Kristin Forbes, and Matthew Luzzetti. 2024. *Quantitative Tightening Around the Globe: What Have We Learned?* NBER Working Paper No. w32321. https:// ssrn.com/abstract=4794370.

Eggen, Mirjam, Hans Gerspach, Eva Hüpkes, Eva Jaisli, Yvan Lengwiler, Renaud de Planta, Rudolf Sigg, and Beatrice Weder di Mauro. 2023. *The Need for Reform after the Demise of Credit Suisse.* Report of the Expert Group on Banking Stability. https://too -big-to-fail.ch/wp-content/uploads/2023/09/Reformbedarf_EN_20230907.pdf.

English, Bill, Kristin Forbes, and Ángel Ubide, eds. 2021. *Monetary Policy and Central Banking in the Covid Era.* E-book published by the Centre for Economic Policy Research, March. https://voxeu.org/content/monetary-policy-and-central-banking -covid-era.

English, Bill, Kristin Forbes, and Ángel Ubide, eds. 2024. *Monetary Policy Responses to the Post-Pandemic Inflation.* E-book published by the Centre for Economic Policy Research, February. https://cepr.org/publications/books-and-reports/monetary-policy -responses-post-pandemic-inflation.

English, William, and Donald Kohn. 2022. "What If the Federal Reserve Books Losses Because of Its Quantitative Easing?" Brookings Institution Commentary, June 1. https://www.brookings.edu/articles/what-if-the-federal-reserve-books-losses -because-of-its-quantitative-easing/.

English, William, and Brian Sack. 2024. *Challenges Around the Fed's Monetary Policy Framework and Its Implementation.* Brookings Papers on Economic Activity, Fall 2024. https://www.brookings.edu/wp-content/uploads/2024/09/1.a_EnglishSack.pdf.

ESRB (European Systemic Risk Board). 2021a. *On the Stance of Macroprudential Policy*, by Stephen G. Cecchetti and Javier Suarez. Reports of the Advisory Scientific Committee No. 11. December. https://www.esrb.europa.eu/pub/pdf/asc/esrb.ascreport202111_macroprudentialpolicystance~58c05ce506.en.pdf?6a01e1d70103ae9845b4891591e 2f4a7.

ESRB (European Systemic Risk Board). 2021b. *A Framework for Assessing Macroprudential Stance.* Report of the Expert Group on Macroprudential Stance—Phase II (Implementation). December. https://www.esrb.europa.eu/pub/pdf/reports/esrb.report_of_the_Expert_Group_on_Macroprudential_Stance_Phase_II202112~e280322d28.en.pdf?2e9 a9e43b97d86e7d933b71fc43efde8.

ESRB (European Systemic Risk Board). 2023. *Stabilizing Financial Markets: Lending and Market Making as Last Resort.* Report by Willem Buiter, Stephen Cecchetti, Kathryn Dominguez, and Antonio Sánchez Serrano. Reports of the Advisory Scientific Committee No. 13. https://www.esrb.europa.eu/pub/pdf/asc/esrb.ascreport202301_stabi lisingfinancialmarkets~3864d5226b.en.pdf?88597d1abb2a887258275ad0a61421db.

ESRB (European Systemic Risk Board). 2024. *EU Non-bank Financial Intermediation Risk Monitor 2024.* No. 9, June. https://www.esrb.europa.eu/pub/pdf/reports/nbfi_monitor /esrb.nbfi202406~2e211b2f80.en.pdf?a9a0bd2000556f5322f99d9afb9a8d37.

Farhi, Emmanuel, and Jean Tirole. 2018. "Deadly Embrace: Sovereign and Financial Balance Sheets and Doom Loops." *The Review of Economic Studies* 85 (3): 1781–1823.

Forbes, Kristin. 2013. "The 'Big C': Identifying and Mitigating Contagion." Jackson Hole Economic Policy Symposium on "The Changing Policy Landscape" sponsored by the Federal Reserve Bank of Kansas City, MO, 23–87.

Forbes, Kristin. 2015. "Low Interest Rates: King Midas' Golden Touch?" Speech at the Institute of Economic Affairs, London, February 24. https://www.bankofengland.co .uk/-/media/boe/files/speech/2015/low-interest-rates-king-midas-golden-touch.pdf.

Forbes, Kristin. 2018. "Macroprudential Policy After the Crisis: Forging a Thor's Hammer for Financial Stability in Iceland." Report prepared for Task Force dedicated to reviewing monetary and currency policies for Iceland. https://www.stjornarradid .is/library/03-Verkefni/Efnahagsmal-og-opinber-fjarmal/Endurskodun-a-ramma -peningastefnu/Macroprudential_Policy_After_the%20Crisis_final_2018_06_03.pdf.

Forbes, Kristin. 2019. "Macroprudential Policy: What We Know, Don't Know, and Need to Do." *American Economic Review, Papers and Proceedings* 109: 470–475.

Forbes, Kristin. 2020. "Inflation Dynamics: Dead, Dormant, or Determined Abroad?" *Brookings Papers on Economic Activity*, Fall 2019 Meetings, 257–319.

Forbes, Kristin. 2021. "The International Aspects of Macroprudential Policy." *Annual Review of Economics* 13 (1): 203–228.

Forbes, Kristin. 2022. "Unwinding Monetary Stimulus in an Uneven Economy: Time for a New Playbook?" Jackson Hole Economic Policy Symposium on "Macroeconomic Policy in an Uneven Recovery" sponsored by the Federal Reserve Bank of Kansas City, MO, August 2021.

Forbes, Kristin, Marcel Fratzcher, Thomas Kostka, and Roland Straub. 2015. "Capital Flow Management Measures: What Are They Good For?" *Journal of International Economics* 96 (S1, July): 76–97.

Forbes, Kristin, Christian Friedrich, and Dennis Reinhardt. 2023. "Stress Relief?: Funding Structures and Resilience to the Covid Shock." *Journal of Monetary Economics* 137: 47–81.

Forbes, Kristin, Joseph Gagnon, and Christopher Collins. 2022. "Low Inflation Bends the Phillips Curve Around the World." *Economia* 45 (89): 52–72.

Forbes, Kristin, Jongrim Ha, and Ayhan Kose. 2024a. "Demand versus Supply: Drivers of the Post-Pandemic Inflation and Interest Rates." *VoxEu*, August 9. https://cepr .org/voxeu/columns/demand-versus-supply-drivers-post-pandemic-inflation-and -interest-rates.

Forbes, Kristin, Jongrim Ha, and Ayhan Kose. 2024b. "Rate Cycles." Proceedings from the ECB Forum on Central Banking on *Monetary Policy in an Era of Transformation*, Sintra, Portugal, July 1–3. https://www.ecb.europa.eu/pub/pdf/sintra/ecb .forumcentbankpub2024_Forbes_paper.ly.pdf.

Forbes, Kristin, and Roberto Rigobon. 2002. "No Contagion, Only Interdependence: Measuring Stock Market Co-Movements." *Journal of Finance* 57 (5): 2223–2261.

Fratto, Chiara, Brendan Harnoys Vannier, Borislava Mircheva, David de Padua, and Hélène Poirson Ward. 2021. *Unconventional Monetary Policies in Emerging Markets and Frontier Countries*. IMF Working Paper WP/21/014.

FSB (Financial Stability Board). 2024a. *Enhancing the Resilience of Non-Bank Financial Intermediation: Progress Report*. https://www.fsb.org/2024/07/enhancing-the-resilience -of-non-bank-financial-intermediation-progress-report-4/.

FSB (Financial Stability Board). 2024b. *Key Attributes of Effective Resolution Regimes for Financial Institutions*. https://www.fsb.org/wp-content/uploads/P250424-3.pdf.

FSF (Financial Stability Forum). 2009. "Report of the Financial Stability Forum on Addressing Procyclicality in the Financial System." April 2. http://www.fsb.org/wp -content/uploads/r_0904a.pdf.

Gagnon, Joseph, and Brian Sack. 2018. "QE: A User's Guide." *Policy Briefs* 18–19, Peterson Institute for International Economics. https://www.deshaw.com/assets /articles/Peterson_Institute_for_International_Economics_Brian_Sack.pdf.

Gopinath, Gita, Pierre-Olivier Gourinchas, Andrea Presbitero, and Petia Topalova. 2024. *Changing Global Linkages: A New Cold War?* IMF Working Paper WP/24/76.

Greenlaw, David, James Hamilton, Ethan Harris, and Kenneth West. 2018. *A Skeptical View of the Impact of the Fed's Balance Sheet.* NBER Working Paper 24687. https://www.nber.org/system/files/working_papers/w24687/w24687.pdf.

Ha, Jongrim, Ayhan Kose, and Franziska Ohnsorge. 2019. *Inflation in Emerging and Developing Economies: Evolution, Drivers, and Policies.* Washington, DC: World Bank.

Ha, Jongrim, Ayhan Kose, and Franziska Ohnsorge. 2021. "Inflation during the Pandemic: What Happened? What Is Next?" *CEPR Discussion Paper* 16328.

Hanson, Samuel, Anil Kashyap, and Jeremy Stein. 2011. "A Macroprudential Approach to Financial Regulation." *Journal of Economic Perspectives* 25 (1): 3–28.

Hartmann, Phillip, and Frank Smets. 2018. *The First Twenty Years of the European Central Bank: Monetary Policy.* European Central Bank Working Paper 2219. https://www.ecb.europa.eu/pub/pdf/scpwps/ecb.wp2219.en.pdf.

Hooley, John, Ashraf Khan, Claney Lattie, Istvan Mak, Natalia Salazar, Amanda Sayegh, and Peter Stella. 2023. *Quasi-Fiscal Implications of Central Bank Crisis Interventions.* IMF Working Paper WP/23/114.

Hooper, Peter, Frederic Mishkin, and Amir Sufi. 2019. "Prospects for Inflation in a High Pressure Economy: Is the Phillips Curve Dead or Is It Just Hibernating?" Paper prepared for the 2019 U.S. Monetary Policy Forum. https://www.chicagobooth.edu/-/media/project/chicago-booth/centers/clark-center/events/us-monetary-policy-forum/2019/2019-usmpf.pdf.

IMF (International Monetary Fund). 2014a. "Staff Guidance Note on Macroprudential Policy." November 6. http://www.imf.org/en/Publications/Policy-Papers/Issues/2016/12/31/Staff-Guidance-Note-on-Macroprudential-Policy-PP4925.

IMF (International Monetary Fund). 2014b. "Staff Guidance Note on Macroprudential Policy—Detailed Guidance on Instruments." December. http://www.imf.org/external/np/pp/eng/2014/110614a.pdf.

Jordan, Thomas. 2021. "The Swiss National Bank's Monetary Policy Response to the COVID-19 Pandemic." In English, Forbes, and Ubide, eds., *Monetary Policy and Central Banking in the Covid Era*, 123–136.

Kashyap, Anil. 2024. "Monetary Policy Implications of Market Maker of Last Resort Operations." Comments at the Jackson Hole Economic Policy Symposium on "Reassessing the Effectiveness and Transmission of Monetary Policy" sponsored by the Federal Reserve Bank of Kansas City, MO, August. https://www.kansascityfed.org/Jackson%20Hole/documents/10443/Anil_Kashyap_Remarks_JH.pdf.

Kashyap, Anil, and Jeremy Stein. 2004. "Cyclical Implications of the Basel II Capital Standards." *Economic Perspectives* 28 (1): 18–31.

Krippner, Leo. 2013. "Measuring the Stance of Monetary Policy in Zero Lower Bound Environments." *Economics Letters* 118 (1): 135–138.

Krishnamurthy, Arvind, and Annette Vissing-Jorgensen. 2012. *The Effects of Quantitative Easing on Interest Rates: Channels and Implications for Policy.* Brookings Papers on Economic Activity, Fall 2011. https://doi.org/10.3386/w17555.

Krishnamurthy, Arvind, and Annette Vissing-Jorgensen. 2013. "The Ins and Outs of LSAPS." Paper presented at the Jackson Hole Symposium on "Global Dimensions of Unconventional Monetary Policy," August. https://www.kansascityfed.org/documents/4563/2013Krishnamurthy.pdf.

Kuttner, Kenneth. 2018. "Outside the Box: Unconventional Monetary Policy in the Great Recession and Beyond." *Journal of Economic Perspectives* 32 (4): 121–146.

Lengwiler, Yvan, and Beatrice Weder di Mauro. 2023. "Global Lessons from the Demise of Credit Suisse." VOXEU Column on Financial Regulation and Banking. September 4. VOX CEPR Policy Portal. https://cepr.org/voxeu/columns/global-lessons-demise-credit-suisse.

Levin, Andrew, Brian Lu, and William Nelson. 2022. *Quantifying the Costs and Benefits of Quantitative Easing.* NBER Working Paper No. 30749. National Bureau of Economic Research. https://www.nber.org/

Levin, Andrew, and Christina Skinner. 2024. "Central Bank Undersight: Assessing the Fed's Accountability to Congress." *Vanderbilt Law Review* 77(6): 1769–1830.

Maddison Project Database. 2023. https://www.rug.nl/ggdc/historicaldevelopment/maddison/.

Ostry, Jonathan, Atish Ghosh, Karl Habermeier, Marcos Chamon, Mahvash Qureshi, and Dennis Reinhardt. 2010. "Capital Inflows: The Role of Controls." IMF Staff Position Note, SPN/10/04. International Monetary Fund.

Romer, Christina, and David Romer. 2024. *Did the Federal Reserve's 2020 Policy Framework Limit Its Response to Inflation? Evidence and Implications for the Framework Review.* Brookings Papers on Economic Activity, Fall 2024. https://www.brookings.edu/articles/the-federal-reserves-monetary-policy-framework-review/

Rose, Jonathan, 2023. "Understanding the Speed and Size of Bank Runs in Historical Comparison." Federal Reserve Bank of St. Louis *On the Economy* blog, May 26. https://research.stlouisfed.org/publications/economic-synopses/2023/05/26/understanding-the-speed-and-size-of-bank-runs-in-historical-comparison.

Setser, Brad. 2024. "The Surprising Resilience of Globalization: An Examination of Claims of Economic Fragmentation." In *Strengthening America's Economic Dynamism,* edited by Melissa S. Kearney and Luke Pardue. Washington, DC: Aspen Institute. https://doi.org/10.5281/zenodo.13973914.

Smith, A. Lee, and Victor Valcarcel. 2023. "The Financial Market Effects of Unwinding the Federal Reserve's Balance Sheet." *Journal of Economic Dynamics and Control* 146: 104582.

Strain, Michael. 2024. "Protectionism Is Failing and Wrongheaded: An Evaluation of the Post-2017 Shift Toward Trade Wars and Industrial Policy." In *Strengthening America's Economic Dynamism*, edited by Melissa S. Kearney and Luke Pardue. Washington, DC: Aspen Institute.

Sun Tzu. Fifth century BC. *The Art of War.* (Citations based on 2018 reprint by Fingerprint Publishing.)

Index

The letter *f* following a page number denotes a figure.

Publisher contact:
The MIT Press
Massachusetts Institute of Technology
77 Massachusetts Avenue, Cambridge, MA 02139
mitpress.mit.edu

EU Authorised Representative:
Easy Access System Europe, Mustamäe tee 50,
10621 Tallinn, Estonia
gpsr.requests@easproject.com

Printed by Integrated Books International,
United States of America